Tales of the Ozark Howler

Saul Ashton

This new edition of Tales of the Ozark Howler is dedicated to the many storytellers in the Ozarks who have taken the time to keep the lore alive, passing it down generation to generation.

CONTENTS

The republication of Tales of the Ozark Howler could not have taken place without the patient stewardship and cooperation of Sophia Ashton, who kept the unique literature of her family alive when so many others sought to see it destroyed. I also owe a debt of gratitude to Allison Weighton for introducing me to this peculiar book and connecting me with the surviving Ashtons. I also wish to thank my ex-wife Cecilia, for the motivation she provided me to see this project through to the end, in the form of her regularly delivered lectures about how any effort related to the Ozark Howler is a fool's errand. I am sure that, without these admonishments, my efforts to see the project through its rough spots would have soon diminished.

- Hawthorne Cornus

FOREWORD

The sad story of *Tales of the Ozark Howler* ought to be regarded as a legend in its own right, although it has sunk to a status quite the opposite of that. The absence of this book from the canon of American folklore is possible only for as long as we hold on to the fears and prejudices that form the shadows of the American character.

I obtained copyright permission, and more importantly, the personal permission of the Ashton family, to republish *Tales of the Ozark Howler* only after the death of the author's final surviving child, Constance. For decades, the Ashton family had held the legal rights to the book only in order to prevent its release, in the hope that it would be forgotten.

They were very nearly successful, but after the death of Constance Ferrell in 2016, Sophia, the daughter of Henry Ashton and granddaughter of the author, patiently negotiated the purchase of all claims to control over legal rights to the book from the surviving members of the family.

It didn't take much money for Sophia to pull this off, as no one else in the family regarded the manuscript as having any value at all. Their parents had depicted it as a frivolous waste of time, and described the man who had written it as a no good godless fool who had put the reputation of the Ashton family in peril.

What Sophia saw when she found a copy of the book amongst the financial records of her deceased aunt was something quite different. She recognized the work as the product of a lively, curious mind and a collection of stories that needed to be told.

When she approached me in the summer of 2017, seeking assistance with the project of republishing her grandfather's book, my first impulse was to dismiss the idea. It isn't uncommon for people to approach me with piles of notes from a dead or aging relative, full of excitement about the idea of converting the notes into a novel or a memoir. Almost always, the notes are confused and inadequate, and the materials is unoriginal and uninteresting to anyone else. Of course, what motivates such proposals is the personal love that people feel toward their own family members, and this motivation is admirable, but cannot be shared with a larger audience.

I assumed that Sophia's project would be the same. I was wrong.

What Sophia showed me was a fully-formed book, edited and ready to be published. In fact, it had already been published, albeit for a very short time, long ago. The material was entertaining, and represented a cultural tradition that had not yet received the attention it deserved.

I didn't understand why *Tales of the Ozark Howler* had been allowed to remain unavailable, out of print for so long. As I spoke with Sophia, it quickly became apparent that she lacked the full story herself. It took months of interviews with the Ashton family and friends, along with searches through family and historical records, to piece the story together.

The reason for the obscurity of this work can be found within the name of its author: Saul Ashton. Saul was not his given name. He was born in 1906 with the name of Paul.

It was in 1928 that Paul became Saul, in a self-transformation intended as a mirror image of the transformation of the Biblical story of Saul on the road to Damascus. In the classic story, Saul was a Jewish critic of Christianity who, as the legend has it, was traveling on the road to Damascus, when he was confronted by the spirit of Jesus, who demanded to know why Saul was persecuting him. Saul apparently didn't have a good response, and so fell to his knees in submission, changing his name to Paul to mark his spiritual transformation.

Like everyone around him in his home community of Hogeye, about 10 miles south of Fayetteville, Arkansas, Paul Ashton was brought up as a devout Christian. Something happened to him as a very young man, however, that provoked him to walk away from the religion of his childhood.

That something may have been Caroline Pearl. Paul and Caroline grew up near each other, but don't appear to have begun to spend any time together until the spring of 1927. Surviving letters between the two of them show an increasing attachment between the two of them as the year progressed. The pair even began, toward the end of the year, to refer to plans for the creation of a family together. It clearly was an intense romantic attachment.

A tragic series of events put an end to that attachment at the beginning of the next year. Records are incomplete, but Sophia Ashton believes that Caroline had become pregnant, and that the young lovers' families did not approve of the couple's plan to marry.

Letter from Paul indicate that it wasn't merely economic unsuitability that led the Ashton family to reject the match with Caroline Pearl. Paul wrote that his affection for Caroline was "not in spite of her darkness, but because of it." His repeated use of this phrase in letters to different friends and members of the family indicate that the theme of Caroline's "darkness" was at the heart of his affection, and of his family's rejection.

The possibility that Paul might have been referring to a metaphorical darkness of temperament is contradicted by his defiant discussion of the racial politics within his own family. "How can we reject Caroline," he wrote, "when our own grandmother was a slave?"

Surviving members of the Ashton family has vigorously denied the existence of any African ancestry within its family tree. However, they have also refused to share the results of any DNA analysis that could confirm their claims of what some Ashton family members refer to as their "racial purity".

Whatever the truth of the Ashton lineage, Paul's belief in the hypocrisy of his family's racism led the young man into fundamental rejection of the conventional, conservative values of his community. By November 2018, he had enrolled as a member of the Communist Party, publicly advocating for revolution under the name Saul.

Although in 1931 he married Felicity McCaul, a choice whose exclusively-European heritage was more ethnically acceptable to his family, Saul did not join his family for its Thanksgiving or Christmas celebrations ever again.

Ashton's interest in the Ozark Howler came as a consequence of his rejection of Christianity, which he referred to as a "deceptive and suppressive opiate". He observed the hostility of local churches to Ozark folk beliefs, especially to beliefs about the Ozark Howler.

The pastor of the Billingsley Church in Hogeye touched on this Christian antipathy toward the Ozark Howler when he declared in a 1926 sermon that, "the Black Howler is nothing more than a servant of the Devil, a lesser demon spreading the message of its masters, tempting us into unholy sabbaths with horned beasts in the darker valleys of our forested hills."

Ashton was intrigued with the tenacity with which this legendary rebel against spiritual norms held on to its place in the imagination of his neighbors, despite official condemnation of it. He began his inquiries into the myths of the Ozark Howler through this lens of religious nonconformity, cataloguing churchmen's diatribes against the beast. A few of the stories included in this book touch upon this theme of Christian backlash against the Howler.

Saul regarded these attacks as a kind of redirection of Christianity's insecurities about its own moral failings. He observed that preachers tended to focus their wrath upon members of their own congregations, who were accused of insinuating a cult of the Ozark Howler into church practices in the name of appealing to local traditions. For Saul, it felt as if Old Testament times had returned, with pastors afraid of the worship of the Ozark Howler as a new kind of Golden Calf.

There's no indication that Saul believed in the literal reality of the Ozark Howler. His repudiation of Christianity in favor of the secular ideology of Communism would suggest that he would reject belief in another supernatural system of belief as well. On the other hand, there is no evidence that he disbelieved the stories about the Ozark Howler, either.

What's clear is that Saul recognized the usefulness of the Ozark Howler as an idea that he could use to counter prevailing cultural norms in his local community, in the Ozark region, and across the Southern United States. "A world in which the Ozark Howler could be roaming the night," he wrote in a letter to the Arkansas Gazette after his book's publication, "is a world in which we acknowledge that there is more to the world than the stories that were told in the Bible."

Saul Ashton's use of the Ozark Howler as a medium for the expression of his resentment against Christianity, and Southern culture more broadly, provoked a great deal of resistance to the publication of his book. Church groups organized protests wherever *Tales of the Ozark Howler* was sold. These protests continue, in a relatively muted form, in the activism of the Society To Obstruct Paganism (STOP), an evangelical group that seeks to censor the teaching of traditional characters of Southern folklore, including the Ozark Howler, but also including the Gowrow, the Snawfus, and the Wampus Cat, in public schools. STOP advocates a "Christ-centered" curriculum in their place.

After Saul Ashton's death in 1938, his own family cooperated with his Christian critics, and withdrew *Tales of the Ozark Howler* from publication. His wife Felicity and their children were by his Communism, his atheism, and his opposition to racial discrimination. In order to rehabilitate the Ashton family's reputation, they not only blocked the sale of the book, but also offered to pay libraries, bookstores, and individuals twice the original price for their copies of the book. All these reclaimed copies were subsequently destroyed by the family. The result was that, within a decade, few copies of the book remained, and most people forgot that *Tales of the Ozark Howler* had ever existed at all.

The stories that were gathered in the book, however, were not forgotten. What Ashton's critics miss is that, as much as Ashton hated the regressive, discriminatory aspects of Ozark culture, he also clearly adored the flavor of life in the Ozarks. *Tales of the Ozark Howler* reads like a love letter to Ozark folklore. Though Ashton's Howler is to be feared, it is also a beloved beast.

This strange approach-avoidance conflict remains in popular perceptions of the Ozark Howler to this day. Though many writers and artists depict the Ozark Howler as a bloodthirsty predator, increasing numbers of fans on sites like Instagram and DeviantArt represent the creature as a friendly, even cute cartoon character. Over the past several years, it has become a trend for young people to adopt an image of the Ozark Howler as a kind of online avatar, an persona of some otherwise inexpressible aspect of their own identities.

This lonesome creature has become us.

So, it is not surprising that, in recent years, the Ozark Howler has become a character in many works of fiction inspired by the ideas first popularized in Ashton's book. Jan Fields plays with the idea of the predator becoming the quarry of human beings in the children's book Hunt the Ozark Howler. In his Mason Dixon series, Eric R. Asher reimagines the Ozark Howler as one member of a bizarre pantheon of Southern monsters confronted by a new manifestation of the Knights Templar.

Missouri Poet Rufus Grey takes a more metaphorical approach to the horned muse, with Ozark Howler Verse, an entire book of poetry dedicated to the beast. Grey writes that, "the Ozark Howler stands for a suspicion that the world holds much more that we commonly give it credit for." This republication of Saul Ashton's neglected work of Southern folklore has been pursued in that spirit.

- Hawthorne Cornus, April 2019

INTRODUCTION

There will be those who, having browsed collections of stories gathered for the entertainment of publishers sitting high on the island of Manhattan, will conclude themselves to be familiar with the folklore of the Ozarks, and feel quite comfortable in dismissing the people of our region as a backward tribe, barely human, and consumed with what they call "tall tales". From this perspective, we are as foreign and as relevant as tribesmen of the East Indies. We provide the urban intellectuals with good material for a quick laugh, or for a doctoral dissertation relating to archaic cultural remnants in the backwaters of America.

Those of us who were born in the Ozarks, who live and will die here, have a different way of looking at things. Looking at a map of our United States, we see New England in a remote corner, and the Ozarks in the very center of it all.

Why tell these stories now? There will be those who think of the Ozark Howler as a relic of the past, as an embodiment of a backwards regional culture unwilling to walk boldly into the future.

To these people, I say this: The future is not what it used to be. A few years ago, American leaders brought us stories of a new generation of progress. For a while, it seemed that we might in fact be moving forward. Exciting scientific advances have improved the lot of many poor families. Women have gained the vote.

In recent years, however, the story of American progress has fallen apart. The great tycoons who claimed to be bringing our nation forward into a brighter future were in fact only operating a kind of confidence game in which they and a small number of their friends were the sole beneficiaries. When the emptiness of their schemes was exposed, and their marketplace fell apart, it was the working man who paid the price. We are still working off that debt, with no end in sight.

Many of us have learned to live humbly, as our ancestors did before us. We have learned to come together and rely on each other in communities, as the promises of the wealthy and well-connected fall apart around us. Where the financial schemes of Manhattan failed us, neighbors down the road will not.

So it is that we have grasped again the simple riches of our land, the birthrights that a decade ago we were ready to forget. We see that the riches of this country are not to be found in the accounts of gigantic incorporated enterprises, but in the forests and fields of America. The achievements that lie ahead of us will not take the shape of more great towers in the cities, but in dedicated acts of cultivation in the countryside, in the settlements never to be seen by the Hoovers and Wilsons of the world.

The Ozark Howler has never been seen by very many people. It is expert at remaining hidden, unappreciated by those whose attention is easily distracted by bright and shining new things.

So, there will always be those who are content to dismiss the idea of the Ozark Howler, saying all too easily, "I never heard of it. It doesn't exist." These are the same people who could not place the Ozarks on a map of the United States. They're the same people who aren't willing or able to recognize the working man of America as a genuine living creature, either. Comfortable shuttling between their urban apartments and suburban "country" homes, they couldn't tell the difference between a pumpkin vine and a potato plant if their life depended on it. Should we depend on such disconnected people to separate what is true and what is untrue?

I cannot show you a stuffed specimen of an Ozark Howler on the floor of a marble museum to prove that the beast is real, but then, I care more for another kind of reality. I care to listen to the stories told by my friends and neighbors. I believe the reports of people who walk the country lanes more than I believe the curators of university exhibits. There is more to this world than what has been dissected and embalmed in the classrooms of Harvard and Yale.

I have studied the lore of the Ozark Howler not because I am desperate to discover monsters in the forgotten corners of America. We have enough human monsters out in the open in our country as it is.

I study the legends of the Ozark Howler because they reveal a way of life that has been almost forgotten in the industrial furnace lands of America. They speak of a connection with the land, of a self-sufficient value in our work, of direct knowledge of the world around us, and a refusal to be owned by any boss, or controlled by any corrupt churchman.

There is a purity I admire in the Ozark Howler. It is at times as terrifying as it is enchanting. We are fascinated with the idea of it, but frightened when we actually encounter it.

Why? Are we afraid of being killed and eaten by this dark, horned beast? I don't think so, not in these times when so many other, more familiar individuals are already bleeding us dry.

I believe that the Ozark Howler is horrifying because it refuses to live the lies that keep the flow of wealth moving efficiently through the arteries of our national body. We see as a monster anyone who does not rely on a manager to make a living. We despise as a demon any creature who does not care to say its prayers before nightfall. We cringe at the beast that makes its home where it finds itself, without any artifice to shelter it from the storms that beset us all.

The Ozark Howler reminds us that we do not have to settle for less, that we do not need to play the games set for us by the banks, that there is a world beyond the workhouse.

It is strange. It is unconventional. However, I count the Ozark Howler as real in a way that no captive tiger in a cage ever could be.

As long as the Ozark Howler roams the forested lands outside of Fayetteville, there is a place where a human being might too be free. A world without a Howler is a world without hope.

So, here in these pages, I record the stories I have found about the Ozark Howler, told in many different voices. Some are told as rumors and reports in local papers. Others are tales told at the edge of firelight for entertainment on dark evenings. Others are mere scraps, documents recovered from schools, from ledgers, from aging accounts moldering in small libraries and small families' dusty bookshelves.

I will admit that there is a lack of the elegance and sophistication that those who claim a love of Literature now require as the price of entry to that glimmering palace known as Publication. Not every story here pretends to cleverness or to the witty turns of phrase that have become fashionable among those who declare their profession to be that of a Writer.

Like the Howler itself, the tales here are hard and grimy to read at times, unpolished, greasy, and tangled. They do not all agree on a single canonized understanding of what the Ozark Howler is, what it looks like, and what it does.

These stories and snippets challenge each other, as they challenge the reader's temptation to construct some idea of what people in the Ozarks believe, what they know, what they have seen of the beast that haunts the wilderness still growing great thickets just beyond the sight of our thick human streets and streams.

The Ozark Howler is no domesticated pet for anyone to own, or even to know with any intimacy. If the Ozark Howler you imagine to see in these pages is not strange and unexpected to you, then you are not yet seeing the Howler at all.

Prepare for your preconceptions to come unstitched.

-    Saul Ashton, October 1936

SIGHTINGS AND STORIES

The items in this section come from stories that I have gathered directly through interviews with people who have had direct encounters with the Ozark Howler, or who know others who have. While these are not word-for-word transcriptions, I have attempted to keep these tales as close to their original form as possible, without resorting to the condescendingly cute alternative folkisms crafted by outsiders who seek to depict the Ozark manners of expression as if they are part of a foreign culture. We speak English as much as, and as well as, people in Connecticut do.

A FAMILY ENCOUNTER

Back around the turn of the century, a man named Jacob lived in Fort Smith, Arkansas with his young family. They were all desperate to get away from the stink of the city for the summer, so they decided to go on a trip out into the hills, content to make camp out in the rough as an antidote to the noise and nonsense they were used to.

Once they got themselves nicely lost on some turning, twisty roads, the family stopped and asked at a roadside restaurant for a place they might stay for a few days. Neighbor talked to neighbor, and by the time Jacob's lunch was done, he was drawn a map to a remote place that would match their needs. By late afternoon, they were happily setting up house in a little three-room cabin that had been there since no one knows when, out next to a gentle stream, for a price that was next to nothing.

"Alright kids, who wants a nice warm fire?" Jacob asked, as his wife Abigail unpacked their provisions.

Ben and Ava, the children, were jumping up and down with excitement,.

"I'll go get some kindling," said Abigail, "Ben, can you come with me to help?"

"Yes, mom," Ben sighed. Ben was the younger of the two children, by six years, and usually accompanied his mother on errands, though he had the feeling that more fun would be had with his father.

"I'll take Ava to go get some bigger firewood," Jacob said. "I think I saw a nicely stacked pile on the far side of the barn."

So, without knowing the territory the pair ventured out into the woods and started to collect some fallen branches, making more noise than you or I could summon on purpose.

Amid the racket, Ben suddenly stopped his work. "Mom," he said uncomfortably, "Did you hear that?"

"Hear what?" she asked.

"Footsteps," Ben answered, "and growling."

"You must be imagining things," said Abigail, not quite believing herself. "Come on let's go back."

Ben grabbed the pile of sticks he had gathered from the ground and ran ahead of his mother.

"Don't get out of my sight!" Abigail yelled, but Ben didn't slow down a bit..

Following around the bend, she came upon her son, standing uncertainly in front of the open door to the cabin.

"Where's daddy and Ava?" asked Ben.

"Ben, drop your sticks and come here right now!" Abigail grabbed the boy's hand and ran to the porch with him, a panicked tone in her voice.

"Where is the food we brought?" she asked, as if Ben would know.

"I don't know mom," Ben said. "It was right here, in the kitchen."

Ben's mother closed the cabin door behind her and locked it shut. She looked out the window toward the barn, but she couldn't see their carriage, and the big door on the front of the barn was lying on the ground, splintered. She was sure it had been hanging securely when she and Ben had left..

"Knife, knife! Where is the knife?" she yelled, fumbling through the kitchen's cabinets.

Ben screamed.

Abigail looked out the window again, and now, standing next to the barn there was a big black creature on four legs, with huge horns on either side of its huge head. It's eyes were looking right at them, and glowing like flames in the gathering darkness.

"Ben, stay quiet, and don't move," she whispered.

She slowly but desperately fumbled around in the strange kitchen drawers for a knife. After seconds that felt like hours, she found a blade, a good half foot in length, and held it firm in her right hand.

"Get away from the window," she whispered to Ben, but it was too late.

"Mommy," he whimpered, "it's coming toward us!"

She quickly pulled Ben from the window and ran with

him into a small, windowless bedroom next to the kitchen, closing its door firmly just as the beast outside reached the porch.

"Too loud," Ben yelled. "Too loud!"

"Hush your voice, and come into the corner behind me, Ben, now!" she yelled.

"It's looking for us? What is it? Is that a bear?" Ben asked.

"That's no bear, Ben." She said. "This thing out there, it's why my father moved us into Fort Smith. It's called the Ozark Howler and I think it knows we're here. I just hope it isn't very hungry."

When she thought of hunger, she usually thought of the way that her husband eagerly ate the meals she prepared for him. This situation was something quite different. A look of fear crossed her face. "Jacob and Ava! They're still out there!"

Just as she spoke her fear, a pair of familiar screams pierced the cabin's thin walls. Abigail restrained herself from returning to the kitchen to see what was happening outside. Protecting Ben was the most she could do. She held him tight with her left arm, and held the knife out in front of them with her right as she backed slowly into a corner.

A loud crash sounded from outside, with what sounded like metal striking metal, followed by the sound of splintering wood. A long strange cry, like the sound of a large, angry pig mixed with the noise of an old steam whistle, came in response.

Abigail and Ben could hear the voice of Jacob shouting, "Go on! Get off!" Then, for what felt like the better part of an hour, there was complete silence outside.

The light streaming in through cracks in the walls had faded away when Ben and Abigail felt the floor shudder with a tremendous thump coming from the direction of the porch.

"I'll protect you," Abigail said to Ben in a voice of cold

determination, but a moment later, it was her husband speaking words of reassurance to her.

"It's gone!" Jacob called in to her. "Let us inside!"

Abigail ran to the front door and practically tore it open, to find Jacob leaning against the wall. With only the light of the moon and stars, she could still see the blood streaming down his face. Behind him stood Ava, apparently whole and unharmed, but with a look of terror in her eyes.

Father and daughter tumbled in through the door to the total darkness inside the cabin. Not one of them dared to venture out the door to bring in the kindling and firewood they had begun to gather before nightfall, so they spoke in chilly blackness of a home they did not know.

Ava told of how she had seen a tremendous beast with thick muscular legs, tangled wooly black fur, larger than the biggest bull she'd ever seen, with horns that would put a Texas longhorn to shame, toss her father to the side like a piece of straw when he tried to stop the creature from killing and eating their horses, tied up and defenseless in the barn. Jacob had little to tell except to share of his own bewilderment and insignificance next to the thing

Abigail told of her father's warnings about the Ozark Howler, of their ancestors dangerous encounters with the shadowy predator. She admitted that she, raised in Fort Smith, had never really believed the tales, had humored her father, but thought them to be nothing more than a quaint and charming bit of local color from less progressive days. She apologized for the danger she had placed them in through her prideful skepticism.

Ben shivered in the darkness, silent.

They found their beds and soft blankets in the darkness, and slept now and then with fearful dreams, waking to the ordinary sounds of nature, threatening them with the return of the beast. After a night worth many nights, the deepwater blue of a promised dawn arrived, with each member of the family looking in the same moment to realize that they had all been standing, watching at the dark windows together, for no one knew how long.

Eventually, there came the moment for courage, when Jacob opened the door again and the family emerged once more into the world outside, waiting to be attacked again. The Ozark Howler did not return, however, and so they left to search for help, for a way back home.

A carriage with no horses was no option, of course, so they walked. The first thing they came across, just a hundred feet down the road leading out of the hills, was a mess of punctured cans and ripped paper packages that had contained their food, strewn across the road before them. The walls of the cabin, it seemed, had been little protection.

It was a long morning's hike before they came to a road well-traveled enough for them to come across another traveler willing and able to help them get to the next town. From there, they hired a ride to take them directly back to Fort Smith, with no more purposeful wanderings through the hills along the way.

Jacob and Abigail never left Fort Smith again. Upon becoming a man, Ben moved to Houston. Ava stayed in Fort Smith until her parents were both dead, and then moved to Chicago. Neither of them have spoken of their encounter with the Ozark Howler since leaving Fort Smith, until now, as this experience was related by Ben.

AN OLD MAN'S VISION

An old man lived in eastern Kansas, a few miles outside of a small community north of Pittsburg, through which a rough road curved like a lazy snake. One day, he came to town to buy candles to get through an electrical power outage, which was more common than a power in-age. As a bonus, the store had its own power generator.

Still, as luck would have it, just as he reached the back

of the store where the candles and matches were to be found, the generator failed as well. It was the early evening, and the faint glow from outside offered little guidance.

Walking forward toward the light, he kept bumping into the shelves, and reached out to feel his way as he heard a howl, not like that of a coyote or a wolf, but something… different. It had a kind of voice to it, but another tone as well, one that was practically mineral. It sounded like the screech of an animal, but also like a metal blade being scraped over an unmoving stone.

Lying still and silent, listening, he heard footsteps approach the front door of the store. He held his breath and lay down on the floor, in the hopes that whatever

approached could not hear him.

After a minute, he heard the thing move into the store, going into the aisle right next to him. The old man planned to run straight out of the store into the street, but his legs didn't run as quickly as they used to. By the time he could manage to stand up, a creature was standing right above him, with glowing red eyes and a menacing snarl.

Instead of running, the old man panicked and heaved with his shoulder, pushing over the shelf that was standing between him and the beast. Finding sudden energy, he ran forward out of the store, knocking over a newspaper stand as he moved forward, causing papers to fly in the air in his wake.

His heart was pounding harder than it had for years, and so the old man stooped over in the middle of the street, his hands on his knees, sure that the creature would be upon him in seconds. Instead, he found himself alone.

After a minute of uncertainty, the old man quietly approached the storefront, looking in through the window to see if the monster had left the store. It had not, but had stopped at the counter where there were baked goods on display. Its hairy, hunched form was leaning over the counter, eating the sweet rolls, oblivious to his presence.

From that day forward, for many years, the store offered that same recipe at a discount to its customers in commemoration of the incident, calling them Howler Rolls in honor of the horrid visitor that came to town.

STUDENTS OF THE HOWLER

One time, two university students came down from St. Louis on a field trip for their zoology class. They had been assigned the task of conducting a survey of journalistic accounts the predators of Missouri.

One of the students, a young woman named Alexandria, was reading through old copies of the Missouri Intelligencer when she found an article about a strange animal called the Ozark Howler. She showed the article to her partner, a young man named Geoffrey, and the two agreed that they should focus their paper on the creature. The pair remained in the library for hours, gathering all the information about it that they could find.

They found out that the Ozark Howler could only be found in the central and western part of the state, far away from the Mississippi River's influence. Geoffrey was nervous about continuing their study, as it would be difficult to gain firsthand knowledge of the creature.

Alexandria pointed out that they had all of their springtime break to finish their project, and suggested that the two of them could be comfortably lodged at her aunt Ruth's house in Rolla, on the northern edge of the Ozarks. Geoffrey reluctantly agreed. He was hoping to spend time with his own family over break, but knew that the project would contribute to his successful completion of his studies.

A week later, the two students arrived in Rolla. Geoffrey was wary of Alexandria's aunt at first, but a pot of tea set his mind at ease. He was further reassured when the elderly woman produced a detailed set of maps of the

nearby hills and suggested a few spots where the Howler might be seen.

"Are you sure that you can make the journey into these remote locations?" Geoffrey asked Alexandria, who was not amused by his protective instincts. "My legs are as strong as yours," she told him, and the matter was settled.

Aunt Ruth offered to pack their lunches for their visits to "the field", and to have warm dinners ready for their return in the evenings. So, with their appetites addressed, the students slept soundly the first night.

The next morning, the pair ventured out into the hills. Their first stop was at the end of a logging road, amid a stand of tall trees. The grass along the roadside was green with the springtime, but did not continue far into the woods, which was already dark with a well-grown canopy.

Alexandria and Geoffrey began their hike into the forest, searching eagerly with their eyes, listening for any unusual sounds, remembering the descriptions of the Ozark Howler they had found in their review of press accounts.

After a couple of hours, they found a small clearing and sat there to eat their lunch. The sun was at its height, making short shadows of the rocks around them, with little space in which to remain cool.

So far, they had been unsuccessful in their search. Geoffrey came up with the idea that his lunch might be sacrificed as a lure for the Ozark Howler. Alexandria was skeptical, but could not come up with an argument against the idea, so long as he was not very hungry,

Geoffrey placed his lunch, a tuna sandwich, on top of a rock in the sun near where they were sitting. They then backed out of the clearing, and hid behind a large fallen tree.

There they waited, hopeful, for hours. For a while, nothing came, but as the sun drew near to the horizon, they heard substantial footsteps coming from the opposite side of the clearing. Geoffrey squeaked with eager anticipation, but Alexandria quickly hushed him.

A large animal with dark, tangled fur and sharp horns walked into the clearing, lifting its snout to catch the increasingly strong smell of the warm fish spread. Seeing the tuna sandwich, the Ozark Howler slowly approached.

Geoffrey scribbled down observations in his notebook while Alexandria brought out her camera to take a picture of the beast, her hands shaking. The Ozark Howler pounced on the tuna sandwich like a gigantic cat leaping upon a mouse, and consumed it in one huge bite.

After making as many observations as they could think to write, the students edged further away from the clearing, into the darkness of the woods, so that their presence would be unobserved by the creature. As they turned to start walking back toward the path that had brought them there, they heard a strange call that sounded like a combination of an elk's bugle and a wolf's howl.

The two made it down the hill in twice the time that it had taken them to walk to the clearing. They spent the rest of the break at Aunt Ruth's house preparing their paper and presentation.

Back in St. Louis, their presentation was the subject of ridicule from the other students, who refused to believe that such a creature could exist just a short drive away from their safe and civilized college walls. Their professor

remained quiet as Geoffrey and Alexandria reported their findings, and motioned for them to join him at his desk as the other students left the room.

"I applaud you for your efforts," said the professor, "as most of your classmates never left this campus to study the animals they claim knowledge of."

"I will grant you a perfect grade for this presentation," he continued, "but provide you with the following advice as well: Abandon this subject of study for something safer. The world of zoology is ready to accept the discovery of a new subspecies of viceroy butterfly, but will reject claims of larger undiscovered creatures, no matter how well documented they may be. It will not do for you to imply that the scientific community has overlooked a substantial beast living in their own backyards. Look to far jungles, not to Missouri, to make your mark."

So it was that the Alexandria and Geoffrey's paper, as well-prepared as it was, was never submitted for publication, and their notes and photographs of the Ozark Howler met the same fate as most students' papers: The garbage heap.

THE CURSED CHURCH OF RUSSELLVILLE

The founders of the Cumberland Presbyterian Church in Russellville, Arkansas were believers in the Ozark Howler, but their new minister was not. Back in 1900, the first service of the church was held under the glowing light cast by a unique stained glass window, the likes of which had never been seen before, and probably will never be seen again.

The window, crafted in fire tones of orange, yellow, and red, depicted Jesus walking through the hills of Arkansas, with a hand raised in benediction toward the Ozark Howler, who bent in pained submission to the savior's spiritual power. The design was the work of Robert Turner, an artisan based in Fayetteville whose work was featured in churches throughout the region. Nowhere else, however, was the Ozark Howler featured in any of his work.

The church had been formed with the support of families who had for generations lived outside of town, but were recently resettled within Russellville proper. They felt that including the Ozark Howler in the design of the new church showed respect to the traditional way of life in the area.

In 1904, a new minister, Horace Greenleaf, made it clear in his first homily that he regarded the presence of the Ozark Howler in his church to be an insupportable abomination. He identified the Howler as a demonic spirit seeking to lead the people of his congregation into damnation. By placing the Howler in a stained glass window, he said, the church had created a new golden calf, the first step in the formation of a new heathen religion seeking to destroy Christianity.

The choir director, Miss Miriam Frawley, led the informal opposition to Minister Greenleaf's anti-Howler program. She wrote and distributed a pamphlet celebrating the window, arguing that speaking to the Howler, reaching its soul, was an embodiment of the mission of the church in its purest form. The pamphlet also asserted that it would not be up to the Minister alone to make decisions about the design and maintenance of the church. The congregation as a whole had to be part of the decision-making process.

The issue came to a head in the Christmas Eve service of 1907, during which Minister Greenleaf declared himself unwilling to serve in the shadow of the Ozark Howler any longer. Seizing a brass candlestick from the altar, he threw it at the stained glass window, breaking a hole in the artwork in the space between Jesus and the Ozark Howler. Miss Frawley and her contingent stood up and walked out of the church in protest, never to return.

At the doorway, Frawley turned, and warned that the Ozark Howler would not allow such disrespect to go unpunished. Under the echo of these fateful words, the few people that remained for the rest of the service suffered from a chilly wind blowing in from outside.

Less than a week later, on New Year's Day 1908, the Cumberland Presbyterian Church burned to the ground, and the stained glass window was destroyed.

While the replacement church, eventually to be renamed the Central Presbyterian Church, was being built, the Frawley contingent of the congregation held prayer sessions outside of Russellville, in a clearing of the woods where they left offerings in a show of peace to the Ozark Howler. However, Robert Turner, the creator of the Howler window, had died, and the church could not find any other artists willing to incorporate the Howler in a new design.

When I spoke to Gladys Hickenlooper, a member of the church's ladies auxiliary board she told me of a similar incident that took place at the St. Boniface Catholic Church in New Dixie, a few miles to the southwest of the Toad Suck ferry on the Arkansas River.

St. Boniface was established just a year after the Cumberland Presbyterian Church in Russellville, and was born into a similar cultural context. New Dixie had a strong contingent of German Catholics, but was surrounded by a sea of Anglo protestants.

The Catholic Church had a long history of incorporating local folk beliefs into its pantheon of "saints", "martyrs", and demons. Father Othmar Wehrlis, the pastor of the new church, was quite comfortable following this practice with stories about the Ozark Howler, but protestants in the area were decidedly set against such acceptance, and began warning about the "satanic" beliefs and practices they believed were being promoted at St. Boniface. They claimed that a secret "black altar" had been established in the basement of the convent next to the church, where abominable sacrifices and other sinister rituals were held.

The fact that the convent did not even have a basement was not considered a relevant fact to those who believed in the dark conspiracy. They claimed that there was, in fact, a secret basement, accessed through a secret entrance.

In St. Boniface's fifth year, a fire was set in the convent building, and quickly spread to the entire church complex. The fire began while mass was being held, however, which made it difficult for the flames to be defeated. It was held to be against Catholic law for a mass to be interrupted once it has begun. So, Father Wehrlis was unable to summon a proper firefighting team for some time.

A crowd quickly assembled outside of the burning church, a rare mixture of Catholic congregants and neighboring protestants, a number of whom gave similar strange eyewitness reports of the disaster. They claimed to have seen a dark, horned beast with glowing red eyes running along the rooftop of the church and convent, spreading the flames wherever it ran. It didn't take long for many in the crowd to identify the beast as the Ozark Howler, and to cast blame on the supposed secret Howler ceremonies, saying that the sacrificial fire in one of those rituals had started the fire, or that perhaps the hellfire brought by the Howler when it was summoned from the Inferno had started the blaze.

The attacks against the churches in Russellville and New Dixie are by no means the first recorded attacks of a terrible black beast against Christian churches. In fact, quite similar church attacks were recorded much earlier, as far back as the 1500s - in Suffolk, England. In the towns of Bungay and Blythburg, two churches were attacked, almost simultaneously, by a gigantic, black-haired creature, a hellhound with glowing red eyes and horns, appearing like nothing so much as the Howler familiar to churchgoers in Arkansas.

There are two possible explanations for this repetition of monstrous attacks against churches by mysterious supernatural animals of similar descriptions. The first explanation is that there actually is such a creature, or a species of such creature, that has a troubled and violent relationship with Christian churches. This beast, if we are to follow this line of logic, would have somehow traveled across the Atlantic Ocean to what is now the Southeastern United States along with European settlers from England, settled in, and then begun attacking churches anew.

The second plausible explanation is that settlers from England who moved through the Southeast into Arkansas and Missouri brought with them a belief in a dark, horned, red-eyed demonic creature that sometimes attacked churches. In this way of thinking, natural accidents leading to the destruction of Christian churches such as those in Russellville and New Dixie became the focus of congregants' superstitious beliefs, embroidered with details of the Ozark Howler's involvement after the fact through elaborations that were either consciously designed or unintentionally made according to cultural presumptions about the causes of church fires.

I will leave it to the reader to decide which of these explanations is the most believable. The larger point which is beyond argument is that the relationship between Christian churches and the Ozark Howler has been anxious, characterized by a strange combination of attraction and repulsion. There appear to be many Christians in the Ozarks who have found a way to accommodate belief in the beast into their religious lives. On the other hand, many of their Christian neighbors regard any acceptance of the Ozark Howler as an abomination and an insult to their religious lives.

No one has, to my knowledge, asked the Ozark Howler how it feels about the Christian churches that now dot its territory. Whatever the Howler's spiritual status, pro-Howler and anti-Howler Christians have sparred for generations.

THE HOWLERS OF PRESTON

The following story was related to me by a young girl who came to my door in the middle of the afternoon on a Saturday, just before I was preparing to take a much-needed nap. She told me that she had heard about my project, and said that she had a tale to tell me, and whether I believed it was my own business. Her manner was very brusque, and it seemed to me that she was pushing me with a purpose – to see how I would react.

I chose to remain clam in the face of her defiance, and suggested that we talk over coffee. She told me the story as you see it below, and her words woke me up long before the dark brew could have its effect. I have kept the tale in her words, as that is how she told it to me.

She had a strange combination of reluctance and eagerness as she began to speak. She did not pause until she was done, except to take a sip of coffee or to catch a breath for a few seconds.

I have not been able to confirm any of the details. I will merely repeat what she said to me: Whether you believe it is your own business.

It was on a bright Sunday, in a town named Preston. My sister Lara and I were the first up in our household, as it was very early, and not a soul stirred in the house.

We immediately made sure to start on the morning preparations. I checked on the little chicken coop that was nestled up near the sidewall, while Lara checked up on storage and prepped the kitchen table for breakfast.

After removing the last egg from under the feathers of Ms. Shall, I was making my way back to the house to assist my sister. Until, as my gaze wandered onto the yard, I spotted it: Of such texture seemed so soft yet sharp at the same time. When I paused to stare at it, I knew of what sort it was. Howler's Bush.

No one knew much of its nature, or why it came to our town. Not even discussed much by older folk, especially in the vicinity of us younguns. Only from the pure luck of one kid overhearing our school masters, Miss Asha and Mrs. Orell, talking while hiding, do we learn anything at all.

Lara and I huddling with some of the boys and girls in the play yard, listening to him rambling on about the strange plant. By some chances, he could have lied for all we knew, but in the least it was something interesting to listen to. From what I can remember, he overheard that, according to Miss Asha, the Winfreys, the most recent family to move here, had spotted a Howler's Bush on their premises, seen first by their young son Hester, while he was playing around under the branches of an oak.

The discussion became silent, but little bits about the plant, and how it was only ten years since if appeared, managed to be heard. Last thing the boy could remember, Miss Asha and Mrs. Orell's discussion ended with a statement like, "Thank God they are Baptist." We made sure not to tell our parents about this, as in some of our families, the punishments could be the harshest.

Up until now, Lara and I didn't know who would be visited next by the bush. Either because it made itself

scarce, or other kids didn't want to tell us about it, there was no more mention of the Howler's Bush since.

From where I was standing, my legs finally found life, and I made my way inside as fast as I can, without joustling the basket of eggs I was holding. When I told my sister what I saw, she told me not to mention it in front of Ma and Pa when they got up. And so, I helped her finish up, until everything was ready. Biscuits were on the table, along with the forget me nots placed above the plates.

Not too long from then, everyone was up, and sitting at the table. After grace, we ate quietly while passing the biscuits around the table. As was a general rule, nobody was to speak during mealtime. Afterwards, everyone went to their rooms to dress for service, except pam who would wait in the kitchen a while before going outside to check on the coop.

Dressed in a faint blue dress, I came down to meet Ma and Lara, and together we stepped out onto the front lawn, where Pa was waiting for us. We were walking up the road when Pa turned his head toward Lara and me and said, "For the rest of the day today, I don't want to see either of you girls in the backyard. You hear me?"

Not daring to hesitate, we both nodded in response. Thought it wasn't clear what the meaning behind such an order was at the time, if I were to guess, my Pa had seen the Howler's Bush. Before too long, we arrived at the front steps of the Baptist Church of Preston. The only church around in these hills of God, of who the shepherd's herd are sane, as said by many, in certain places of town. we went in, and joined the families already seated in their rows.

Finding a seat, I sat down next to Lara, with the aisle to my right side. From what I can remember of the inside, it was a simple rectangular shape, with pinewood benches, and light oak floor planks. Sunbeams hit the white painted stone wall behind us, short of touching the archway from under which we entered. And the beams of light, as they were visible in contrast to the shadows of the room, could be traced back protruding from a window, shaped as a downward facing crescent. Below, a lonely podium where behind patiently stared Reverend Granger.

There was a period of silence, as it was traditionally done every Sunday, while we waited for everyone to come in. This time, it was Mrs. Orrell's family, quietly closing the doors behind them before walking down the aisle to take a seat.

I was waiting, impatiently swinging my legs as I continued sitting. Noticing this, my sister held my hand firmly, and I stopped. Then, the church bell rang, loudly, only once, echoing in the hills outside.

Service began, and Reverend Granger formally greeted us. Reciting a hymn, of which I can't recite completely, other paid most attention, except for Pa, who Ma would keep in every service for as long as she could. At a glance, he had an aura of disengagement, most clearly seen in his eyes.

After reciting the hymn, Reverend Granger thanked us all for coming, told us that we're in the sights of God today. Following that was the same saying spoken almost every Sunday. He said to everyone, "To all who have just become a sighter, fear not the Bush of the Howler, for you are all children of God and every Ozark Howler his servant," in which we all gave an amen.

As if on cue, Pa got up to step silently outside, despite Ma's glares. As he seemed not affected, Reverend Granger reached under the podium itself. I was surprised, for usually the cross was only brought up on occasion for holidays, or funerals. Being brought up now, of all days, I was confused. When I looked around, kids I'd go to school with appeared the only ones to share what I felt.

Looking at the bronze arms, extending out from a bright stone in the middle of the cross, I knew something different was happening. What happened next broke my young mind. Reverend Granger opened his mouth, absent of voice, and everything thing changed.

Where there had been dozens, there were far fewer remaining. Most of them were young, with some I recognized. My sister was still with me, still holding my hand. We were no longer sitting, but standing, and the church was darker than before. Reverend Granger was there too, with his mouth still open. After a moment, he turned to us, and his voice returned, echoing around the room. He welcomed us, said he was glad we could come, and called us "sighters".

The room continued to darken, to the point where I could barely see anything at all, except for the contained pale light in the crescent, and Reverend Granger's face, illuminated by the square cross still in the podium, which seemed to glow. Everyone in the shadows was silent.

I could still feel Lara's hand, but she too was quiet. I could only see Reverend Granger's frozen face, and yet hear his voice continue speaking. He told us how God loves us, but how his servants are more demanding. He said that as the Ozark Howlers watch over us, they miss their old hills they called home, and as they've settled into our mountains, they made a demand to God that a gift be given to them.

"…and so, people were called to this exact hill, told by visions that it will be their home. Then came the birth of this town, and church, away from those not worthy of God's true love. As we've prospered, God's love only grew. The Ozark Howlers, waiting for us, they grew to love us too. And gift has been provided."

It was getting warmer, and warmer, and though I couldn't see completely, the shape of the roof and walls seemed to be slowly changing before my eyes, as Reverend Granger continued on. "Going on a long journey, you need to root yourself when finding a new home. As so with the guardians, they need new bodies to fill. As servants of our Lord of Heaven - no more! A reward for our true faith, we will be filled by the spirits of the Ozark Howlers, and become them."

The chamber contorted and convulsed, each board and brick of stone moving in a mysterious pattern. Before long, the crescent burned into a dark gold color, with rays of light finding their way back into the room, brightening whatever was left of the church into a haunted glow, revealing about a dozen others.

I tugged on my sister's arm. "We should go," I said. "We don't belong here!"

It was getting hot, the smoldering warmth with the golden light. Sweat trailing down my back, I could have mistaken myself in being in the heart of a bonfire. I tried to tell the Reverend to stop, but to no avail, as he picked up the square cross from the podium and moved his eyes to me.

"Don't worry, child. Rejoice instead of panic, and join with the others. Let go, and join in our salvation." He turned his gaze to the object he held in his hands, lifting it to level with his face.

I was petrified. No Ma, no Pa, no remainder of Preston in this place. I looked up at Lara, but she was not there, no sign of my sister, of her soul.

"Do not despair, sighters, the rest of us, however blessed, aren't as lucky as you."

Reverend Granger brought the cross closer to him, so close that I couldn't see his face.

"The cross picked you all, my children. Hold tight to your faith, for while the others will not join you in your journey, rest assured you will live on in Heaven, in the sacrifice you will all burden. Let go."

With that, the cross ate his face. Encompassing his head, the crunch of bone and tooth could be heard. To the best I could understand of everything around me, however I believe Reverend Granger left us.

The being standing in his place, a demon, finally broke me down. I had to leave this place. It was too much. Never mind about my sister, for I knew she was gone, too. I twisted my hand in her grip, struggling and twisting with my hand now laced with beads of sweat running down my arms.

Hair, dark as crows, sprouted from around the cross, covering the arms, living the stone visible in the center of its head. It swung its neck, expanding into something that was... animal, but couldn't be understood, uncomprehended, a sight never seen on this Earth.

I turned my head away. I couldn't see it for another moment. I had to leave. I continued with my hand, as I could feel Lara's loosen, and I was free.

Hearing its movements, I glimpsed its legs loping around the room. I sure made to avoid it, and moved to the edges of the room, feeling around what I assumed were walls. All the while, I could hear each body, one at a time, going down its gullet.

I couldn't panic. I had to keep going. I don't know when it got to what remained of my sister.

Hands continued searching the wall, and then I found it. I turned the door handle, but before I could push, the smell of musk surrounded me. One hand on the door, I

turned to see its face, the stone bright, and the only thing beautiful about the beast.

It craned its head forward, and looked into me. What could only have been lips sprouted from the mat of fur. I stood so still in that moment.

From the lips, it spoke to me. "Give me a kiss, darling."

My foot moved backwards, and before I knew it I fell backward through the doors of the church,

which quickly closed. And there it was, intact.

I got up and looked around. Everything was quiet. Everything was normal, except for the circle of Howler's Bush surrounding the church.

I started walking, away from the church, yet still in the circle. I crossed over a bush, and then suddenly I became dizzy, stumbling over myself until I collapsed onto the dirt road.

Then, I dreamed. In the dream, I got up and looked behind me, to see the church I had emerged from turn itself into a clawed hand. It wanted me, and so I ran.

It tore down the trees close to where I stood. I ran through Preston, and as it reached for me it destroyed the homes and shops that stood there, too. It tore down the school. It trampled the small fields.

But, no matter how close it was behind me, I wasn't caught. As the ground sloped downwards, I was running down the hill, a trail of destruction following.

Before long, I tripped, and tumbled down the rest of the way, until I stopped at the bottom, in a muddy river bank which cushioned my fall. The claw could not follow, for it could not quite reach me.

Then, in a fit of rage, the claw stampeded to the top of the hill, where dirt soon flew down, covering me and filling in the river. And there was howling, loud and terrible from the hill, from the heart of which sprang monsters.

Then, the dream ended. They said they found me in the woods, half covered by dirt.

It's been years, and yet here I am, writing about what I want to forget. I didn't tell anyone about this, not even Auntie Georgina.

For all I know, none of it could be real. According to them, there was never even a nearby town by the name of Preston.

I wanted it to be true, and so I believed it for quite a while. Until I saw something while I was outside. Only for a bit, I told myself, and off I went.

It happened the I was on a field's edge. I was gazing at the wheat, moving to the wind, when I spotted a dark, still figure to my left. Moving closer, I made out the horns, peaking from the top, along with ears, and a long tail swishing in the air.

I was getting close, but I didn't stop myself, until I was standing a short distance in front of it. I needed to see.

Neither I nor the Ozark Howler moved for some minutes. Finally, it lifted its head from the wheat.

On my life, I swear I saw my Pa's wide eyes looking

back at me. This was today.

THE SACRIFICE OF ROCKY COMFORT

There is a new generation in the Ozarks that, while born to the hills, feels an estrangement of them, as if the land is no longer theirs to claim, a failed inheritance. I met a young man of this generation as I was organizing my notes for this book. This man, Dennis Murphy, though he is the son of a farmer with century-old connections to his country, is now a profession with an ambition of teaching the lore of the Ozarks in the Ozarks, as if it is of equal importance to the legends of old England or Ireland.

Mr. Murphy has talked to me – several times – of his dream of writing an epic poem of the Ozarks that would match the scale of the Odyssey of the Greeks, but tell the stories of the hill country instead. One of these stories he seeks to include in his great work is the one told below. He insists that it is based on events that actually took place, just as many scholars tell us that Greek sailors really lay siege to a city named Troy thousands of years ago.

A short poem by Murphy is also included in a later section in this book, of poems about the Ozark Howler.

When pioneers crossed the Mississippi and cleared farmsteads for themselves from thick forests using nothing but their muscled arms and sturdy steeds, they brought with them their cherished beliefs. Still, no churches could be built in the sparsely populated frontier. The toil of making a home in the wilderness was all consuming.

So it was that these early settlers mixed in with the people who had already lived on the land, learning their ways, both practical and spiritual. Though they remained Christians, these farmsteaders adopted some practices that did not fit the orthodox theologies enforced in the larger cities.

They adapted, and made the most of the reality they were faced with. That reality included the need to keep the Ozark Howler, which early generations called the Hoo-Hoo, for the sound it made, or the Nightshade Bear.

The Nightshade Bear, they explained, was a hungry

creature unlike any other. It could not be blamed for its appetites. It was not evil in a religious sense.

So, the pioneers and their Indian neighbors developed a kind of Communion With The Land that allowed them to continue developing the territory in peace. Like the classic Christian Communion, this new Communion of the Ozarks required a sacrifice.

So it was that when the harvest was complete one year, Edward Brixy, the eldest member of the Rocky Comfort settlement, went taking his yearly walk amongst his neighbors, looking for the stoutest amongst all the children, one whom, though yet tender, was also of an adequate size. This would be the child taken to the Rock of Comfort, the great stone rising out of the land that made them safe.

It was tradition, standing as long as any of them ever cared to think about, to leave a child there on this night in mid-November, made sleepy with a sweet blackberry wine, with his body wrapped tight in ropes to prevent a getaway. In the night, the child would be left tied up on the rock. In the morning, the child would be gone, except for a little bit of blood, and the rain would clear that away soon enough.

Never since this annual sacrifice had been held were the people of Rocky Comfort made the victims of the Nightshade Bear in any other way. None of its people were taken. The livestock of the settlement were likewise left to fatten themselves in the fields in peace.

It was not, in truth, a comfortable arrangement. No one ever forgot the price of their accord with the Hoo-Hoo. Yet, it had been comfortable enough to be maintained.

Old Man Brixy was beginning to feel differently about it this year, though, for at every home he visited, he received the same answer to his inquiry: "Children we have, but none as stout as your Samuel." No reasonable argument could be made in reply. Samuel Brixy was now on the far end of fourteen, and had been growing at a pace no one had ever seen before. He was already as tall as his father, and yet, he still had just a touch of a young boy's softness about him.

Samuel was the perfect choice the choice that must be made, and yet, with every home that he came to, Edward grew in his resolve that this year, that choice would be different. So it was that, when the round of visits was complete, and the fathers of the settlement gathered outside of the Brixy house, no child was offered.

"This year," Brixy told his neighbors, "We will end it."

The men were furious. Year after year, their children had been sacrificed to the beast, abandoned as fresh meals. Now, when it was Bixby's turn, why should it be different?

Yet, Brixy was canny. He appealed to the courage of his neighbors, asking if they would, at long last be men and defend what was theirs. Well, how could they say no?

It was then that Edward Brixy shared his plan. "I'll need the biggest buck and the most venomous snake you can find." By sundown, a great big cottonmouth as tall as any man in the crowd and a buck with widely branching antlers were brought to his front porch.

The men sliced open the deer's gut, then cut the head off the snake and squeezed its venom into the belly of the buck. They then decapitated the deer, and cut off the lower half of its legs, skinned it, and stitched its body back together. Next, they wrapped the deer in an old blanket, which they doused with the same blackberry wine they had used in previous years to put their own children to sleep. Finally, they took the deer carcass up to the Rock of Comfort, and tied it there in the same way they usually did.

In ordinary years, the adults living in the area around the Rock would drink themselves to sleep on the night of the sacrifice. This year, they stayed sober and awake, listening for the sounds of the arrival of the Nightshade Bear.

Each house heard it in a different way. Some heard the soft but unmistakably rhythmic padding of heavy feat through the fields and forests. Others heard the ripping of the ropes holding the dead dear to the rock. They all heard what came next.

The Hoo-Hoo ran through the night screaming, not with the mighty bellow it once had, but with a terrible howl that made it sound as if the creature was ripping out its own lungs with each painful cry. In its fury, it circled around and around the rock in ever-widening arcs, smashing into trees and wagons, tripping over its own feet as the agony of the serpent's venom coursed through its veins.

That is how the Nightshade Bear was changed, and how it became the Ozark Howler we hear today. The venom did not kill the creature, but it warped it somehow, either by burning its throat or by ripping a gash in its soul, so that ever since that night, the beast calls out at night in a voice full of painful malice, but stays clear of human beings, as it learned its lesson well.

Some say that's now how the story really goes. As some others tell it, the Hoo-Hoo really was killed that night. The poison surged through its body almost instantly, and the monster fell over right next to the Rock of Comfort.

According to this version, the people who had settled nearby took their vengeance out on the Nightshade Bear. As it had eaten so many of their children, they in turn roasted the monster on a gigantic fire in front of Edward Brixy's home. Every settler, man, woman, and child, was served a hot, steaming plate of Hoo-Hoo.

The terrible mistake of this meal was revealed to the less-hungry settlers, those who held back from taking a bite before their meal cooled down. They watched their friends, neighbors, parents and children writhe in agony before dying, as the still-vital venom of the cottonmouth snake surged through their bodies until they were cold and dead.

As this story tells it, the Ozark Howler that we hear of today in the remote hills and valleys of our countryside is the ghost of the Nightshade Bear, still furious at its murder, but howling triumphantly at its own revenge against those who had the audacity to hunt the hunter.

The Rock of Comfort became the social center of the settlement of Rocky Comfort, Missouri, even as the memory of the confrontation with the Nightshade Bear faded from the awareness of all but the oldest residents. This great stone remains there today, though you won't see it, as it rests underneath the foundation of the small Baptist Church that is the one place for Christian worship in the settlement.

ARCHIVAL DOCUMENTS

The following items are references accounts of encounters with the Ozark Howler found in papers at the College of the Ozarks, formerly Arkansas Cumberland College. Further details of their authors' biographies are not available.

A WARNING

When waking up today, I thought for certain that the day would be uneventful. Same room, grits and eggs for breakfast, same familiar landscape; nothing new. That is not to say that it's bad. Deep down, I needed this type of place. Being here as part of my new life is better for me, without disturbance or the noises.

Occasionally, a far off neighbor would come by on the road, and give a polite greeting my way, before moving onto their own business. To their knowledge or not, I appreciate the peoples' understanding in this area. For the years I've been here, the citizenry has made themselves so scarce, they may as well not exist, which I love them for, along with less noise.

In my head, I was sane. When I went out this morning, I was happier. Walking out into the woods at the foot of the mountain, I was happy, and it was quiet. Just a regular, non-eventful day. The forest understood what I needed, and so remained calm and peaceful. Even the surprise the land gave to me was quiet.

Their thick fur, beautiful tails, the color of their eyes resembling that of a blood orange, surrounded by silence as I approached them. Such little things, at first I thought, have come as a sign that my roots have dug down enough to be secure. Of course, the forest didn't like me, as I soon found out when inspecting its gift.

To my horror, the tiny devils in disguise turned into immature deformities; over-sized snouts with jagged teeth peering out from their lips, disproportionate limbs, and multiple discolored growths sprouting from their heads were beholden to my sight. It started getting noisy.

Any sign of life from their forms was absent, until one of them clumsily stepped forward, and uttered the most disturbing sound made, of such loathing, in what I'm sure was a curse of the non-verbal manner. As was apparent when I fled back here, to my home, but with the noise chasing behind me. It was a trap, an unkind joke that everything here has unloaded onto me, waiting for a sign of my contentment. To conclude, this place is not for me, and nor should it ever expect to see me here, ever.

I leave this here to warn against any further settlement into this cursed place,

Darleane H. Madice

A FACE IN THE LANTERN LIGHT

Before I go on, I want to make it clear that I'm just writing down an honest account of what I saw, along with my best explanation for what it was. Whether anyone believes this is up to them, but to me this was a very real experience. It started 3 months ago, this year being 1927, when I was making my trip to move in with an uncle of mine. I was attending Rhodes College, which happened to be located the next state over from where he lived. After beginning what was the second year there, pursuing my finance major, I fell out of love for that field, and dropped out of that place.

Not having the courage to face my parents after that, I needed to go somewhere where I could collect myself and think. Knowing my uncle from when I was young, along with the fact that he happened to live the closest, he seemed like the best candidate. I contacted him about my situation, and soon after that I was taking a coach with my things back west, past Little Rock. It was getting a little dark we I continued on the road I was on. Eventually I was let off at my turn in the road and walked north towards my destination.

Around half an hour later, I was on a thin road, barely wider than a footpath, completely surrounded by dark forest, when suddenly a large dark figure jumped across the road in front of me. I was alarmed, to say the least, and immediately stood still to consider what I had seen, wondering if I should investigate. Stepping forward slowly, I looked around the side of the road for any sight of movement or sound.

As my eyes were adjusting to the dark, I thought I could see a large, looming figure atop of a rise, around what I estimated to be a few yards from where I stood. I didn't know what to make of it, seeing only the still outlines of the silhouette.

I noticed it slowly moving towards me, which gave me enough reason to hurry forward on my way. I knew that I still had about two miles to go before the nearest neighbor who might let me in. Before I began walking again, though, I lit my lantern so that I could see the way more clearly. That's what I told myself, anyway. I think I just felt safer with a light, as if the brightness would protect me from the creature in the darkness.

I began to see more clearly at the edge of the warm light what I could only describe as a somewhat feline face, but with dark and long shaggy hair, as well as large yellow eyes that were focused on me. Without thinking why, I thrust my lantern out in front of me, before the creature could get any closer. With my heart beating fast, I began walking down the road again as fast as I could.

It followed. I am sure of that, but the beast never attacked. The last I saw of it when I pressed on the gas was a blur, followed by a guttural howl as I quickly put distance between us. Shortly after, I arrived safely at my uncle's.

After greeting him in his driveway, along with exchanging other pleasantries, I told him about what just happened. With a curious expression on his face, he told me that during my stay, I should watch out for big cats in the area, as that might have been what I've come across on the road. After that, I got settled into his place, and became very grateful for his generosity and good-will in the next few weeks I stayed there. During that time, I did keep my eyes out during the daytime, but I didn't spot anything unusual during my stay. The only bit that was in any way uncanny was one time, when I was in bed and heard a far-off howl that sounded strangely familiar. Then again, I could have imagined that bit, as I wasn't fully conscious then.

As you could guess, I wasn't convinced that all I saw that night was simply a cougar. That thing was pretty big for a regular mountain lion, not to mention its long fur, and oddly shaped face. During my stay, and after, I looked around for any books and old newspaper copies to see what I could find on reported creatures in this area. It took me around 2 months before I eventually did find some useful sources that at least gave me some idea of what I saw out there.

Ranging from the southern Appalachians to the

Ozark mountains, there was a legend of a creature called the Wampus. It is described often as having the half-dog/half-cat appearance, being able to run on all fours or erect. The origins of this creature were hard to exactly pinpoint. The best I could come up with is the area of Georgia/ North Carolina, in pre-colonial times. According to the Cherokee, a tribe originating from that area, the creature's abnormal form somewhat resembled a mountain cat, with yellow eyes that can drive men mad. Here in the Ozarks, there have apparently been some more recent accounts that claim people have seen the Wampus around bodies of water, or in the woods.

While reading more into this, there were references on a couple of somewhat local records, about a similar creature that's called the Ozark Howler. Also described as cat/dog like, along with some bear-like features as well as small horns, this reported creature's howls are said to have been heard around the Ozarks on occasion. It was very hard to come across anything relating to this beast, let alone very few having reported to actually seeing this thing, giving me the assumption that it's rare to come across. Personally, I think these two unusual animals are one in the same, and the descriptions best fit what I saw. Coming to this conclusion, I am definitely going to be on guard when passing through the area in the future. Despite the risk, however, I don't think I'll ever get to see what I saw ever again in my lifetime.

A GOODYE

Samuel, I pray that you go to heaven and look at me and that it's fun. I wish I can play with you and that you can live again and we can be happy, and I can pet your horns. You are the best Ozark kitty I have found, and I love your howl. I always loved you, and I know you love me too.

Goodbye Samuel, I will miss you.

THE JOURNAL OF F. SMIT

Speaking as a resident of Oklahoma, life here isn't the kind to give anyone a jump from the fence. Living here to some means being a living embodiment of the humid summers and livestock gorging on the dry grasses. As a farmer, you wake up and tend to what needs to be done in the farmyard and field, going at a constant pace from dawn to dusk, before settling down and waiting to do the same thing over. Farmers in the western parts of this state always manage to plow through, and attend to the chores day after day. I suppose there's certain pride in the work, as certain folks see in their condition means for carrying themselves high. But, however appealing the repeat of labor and seasons appears, I cannot settle for minor distraction over the dull life I was living.

Unlike most of the state, where I live is a more forested area in the middle of almost absolute solitude, with the nearest town, Big Cedar, miles away. When I mentioned that life here isn't the kind to give many if any a shock, I mean it especially for where I live. Here, there is not much farmland to settle, nor the constant urban activity to surround yourself with. The only thing here that keeps me from up and going somewhere else is the wonderful nearby mountains, which in every hike up to summit for me has given bewildering views of the mountain range and valley. Not mention an appropriate amount of game, come the right time of the year, which does provide for rare excitement.

As a newcomer from the east, this was reason enough to establish my home here. But, as I grew accustomed to daily life in the land, days only became more tiring and especially humid, until I would move around with lacking purpose and excitement.

Everything more recently changed against that way of things when news came locally of a sheepherder, a little to the west of Big Cedar, looking for men to help after losing several sheep to a possible coyote or cougar. Seeing as this is a better opportunity than nothing, I shortly made sure to travel down and make myself available. Knowing a little of the local folk, I knew there'd be plenty of men and boys waiting to prove themselves useful, which upon arriving I was not disappointed. No doubt pleased, the landowner stationed the boys along the fences to keep a lookout, while the rest of us were given leave to explore the nearby fields and forests.

Finding the remains of some sheep near the property, it was largely believed to have been a cougar. Based upon that, I along with the others spread out to better have a chance of finding what killed the sheep. On my own, I spent many hours making my way through the forest at around the base of the mountain that was close to the actual property. Nothing much happened for the day, besides startling a buck and a couple of coons while walking. Being disappointed by the typical lack of activity, I decided to head on my way back to sheepherder's homestead.

I was still on my way back, walking through thick brush for about an hour past dusk, when I suddenly heard a faint, low growl coming from my right side. Being alert, I could only quietly turn towards where the growl came from and listened. After a minute of standing around, I finally heard a rustle in the bush in front of me before a dark figure quickly leapt from hiding at me. In complete and utter surprise I shot off a single round from the rifle I was carrying, before falling on my back with the thing's weight on me The thing was large and cougar-like, with black fur, and what I remember to be dark yellow eyes focused on me as its claws dug into my sides. Instinctively I tried protecting the front and back of my neck against its jaws, which kept trying to get past my arms by biting them rapidly. All the while my sides felt like they were about to be torn about by the claws sinking deeper into my skin.

For what felt like a while it went like this, until the beast turned its attention away from my neck, and fastened its teeth into my skull. Feeling nothing but blinding pain and panic, I could do close to nothing as I was pinned, waving one arm not protecting my neck around feebly. At any moment I could have died with my skull crunched by the beasts jaws, if not for a bullet hitting one of its legs. Followed by a yowl of pain, the abnormally large cat let me go and fled as a couple of other shots were fired in its direction. Soon after, the man who fired those shots rushed towards me as I was bleeding out.

Barely conscious at this point, I was brought back to the homestead, helped by that man who I soon recognized to have been one of the volunteers scouting out the area. I later learned that his name was Doug, and that he happened around when he heard me fire my gun, which caught his attention and sent him running in my direction. To put it quickly after that, I don't remember much else, other than I was treated by a local doctor who was sent for by one of the boys stationed at the fence. It took a while, but I did recover from my injuries, and am currently alive. Reflecting back, I hated myself for looking for such reckless excitement, with the lack in experience hunting dangerous game, such as what attacked me out there.

Now, I take it upon myself to not go out in the woods during nightfall, for fear of encountering any other unsavory beasts waiting. In the end, I got what I wanted. So for the time being, I plan to live content with my life, and safe. This is what I can recall concerning the attack and myself before then.

May future generations make more sense out of this than I ever could,

F. Smit

THE LOST LOG OF GRACE

What follows are the surviving portions of the travel log of Teddy Grace. The previous pages in his journal were either lost or too damaged to remain legible.

Entry 36

This is my 23rd week walking down, wake 'til rest, spanning 16 miles at least in my estimate of the last 9 hours. To recall my current progress, I'm a month's long trek south from the Black Hills excavation site. Supplies have dwindled down concern ably. The horse is fed at least and so far hasn't died on me yet. Second day out of the territory, and now, as it seems, I appear to have fallen onto lands of the great Mississippi shore. By stroke of luck, I should find myself a ferry down to New Orleans, if I continue along the shores far enough. Pray I don't starve, and God guide me a swift journey to safety. Before I settle for the night there is an object I must attend to.

Entry 37

Third day of trekking down the Mississippi. Surprisingly remote, and noticeably darker for the season. Adding to the dreary state of myself, this marks the first day of no food. Don't have time to fish, for time does pass quickly. Horse fed. 24 miles of the last two days or so. Got to find that ferry. That's the only thing that matters. Just now checked, and it is so. The acquired object is safe. in the morning, gotta gallop down the river. I must catch my way down to New Orleans. I have no room for anything but that objective. I've had enough of this.

Entry 38
Another day gone by, and I wouldn't have hesitated to feast myself to this parchment. 24th week walking down, and more walking tomorrow. When morning bird called this morning, my luck came back, upon discovery of a couple of settlements a few hundred yards from where I was standing at a fork in the widening river. God given, these souls saved me from my insanity of hunger. I am alive, and am fed, Horsie too, and so far hasn't died on me yet. The object is with me, but I can't seem to have remembered the name yet.

Just now, I've been informed by my hosts of a close docking point at a town a few miles. I will make sure to thank them eventually before my mind blacks out.

Running rivers filled my ears as I lake next to the window. Complete silence, save for the eyes in the window, and the whispers in my dreams.

Entry 39
Accompanied by a man of the name Martin, I have made my way to where I am now. God bless his soul, and God bless that my journey ends soon. Waiting on the docks, my supplies replenished, horse food, along with it being safe.

The ferry appears damaged. With such thing my luck is running out, and I need to get out of here.

I don't remember sleeping, but I woke up in a room at Harriots Inn. Everything is here with me, except for the horse. Poor soul I don't understand it, but last I remember, I was riding out of town. Maybe I'll remember tomorrow, at which point repairs should be made. New Orleans can't wait for me.

Entry 40

Few days past, marking 25th late week for me. Now repaired, the ferry has been moving swiftly on the ever widening Mississippi. From my cabin, I cheer. New Orleans, I come to you.

Entry 41

Being on a tight vessel, there isn't space to walk. Not enough room to conversate, as people here are terribly dull. In my attempts, the best thing I leaned was only the month it is now. It is April. Now I know. It is now decided, I will remain in my cabin. With exception to food served this evening.

The food is disgusting.

Entry 42

It has grown dark in my cabin. In the care of my wellbeing, this is the perfect place for insanity to grow. But I don't like going out. I don't like the eyes on the shore, and I won't touch the door if there's whispering behind it, possibly. The Back Hills, it seems, have not decided to let me go.

Entry 43

I woke up to see Andrew at the foot of my bed. He was the best digger on the team. Of course, what astonished me the most was how much dirt remained on his clothes. He clear as day didn't stop to bathe on his way here. Putting that aside, he was a friendly face then, very different to how he was when he looked at me. We didn't talk much. Very quick. Concerning what we said, I remember congratulating him on getting this far, to him that was ridiculous. He's apparently lying somewhere in Alberta, at the edge of a farm. Now, he says, he wanders wherever he pleases. Couldn't help but laugh. Knowing him, being the uptight sort, he didn't laugh with me. Last thing I can remember, Andrew seemed to be upset. He got up, and the last thing he said to me was to be aware, Ezzy is outside my room, and that I should know he has fallen to the kitties. Then he left, opening and closing my door. As the door was closing shut, I saw something. Thank you, Andrew.

Entry 44

It is wonderful. I don't know how old it is, for despite the smoothness of its copper center, it has an ancient presence. This is my first time noticing, and I don't know why. I can't do anything today but look at it. The carvings are a thing of beauty. Of more sophistication than I thought its makers were capable of. And New Orleans is only a day away.

It is glowing, red and gold, the copper centerpiece seeming to turn with the continuation of my gaze upon it. Whatever light is upon it, I know for sure it isn't the cause of it. Then I know for sure it was in fact a gift, to the Indians blessed, given by their gods.

Entry 45

Of some things made, they shouldn't be given to the mortal world. It gave me dreams last night, of Harriot Inn. Best I can describe, a severed horse head was worn by a tail, and looked in my room. Only I wasn't sleeping. I walked to the window, and looked to the street. There I saw the tail's body, that being of a dark hairy monster. Moving on from the bulk of the body, I saw

Ezzy's head turn up to face me. He was different. Aside from most of his head being covered by dark fur, the two long horns at the top had me captivated. His mouth was moving, too. I was too far up to hear him but I could tell he was talking to me. The horned monstrous freak was talking to me, and seemed to smile the more I watched him, and the more that impossibly long tail made my horse's head nod.

The horse is dead, and now I am a cursed soul. God help me, the mist has finally lifted from that part of that memory. Riding out of that town, but to run back to it. I am beginning to understand why it was buried, given back to the demons in the ground. The ground from which we took it.

Ezzy has stopped whispering from behind the door, but I'm no fool.

Entry 46

This morning, I opened the door, and nobody was there. Wherever it went, I have not been sane recently. I am glad to leave the ferry, with Ezzy on it.

So I thought I found peace, but I am proven wrong. I hired a cab immediately. I looked back only to see Ezzy loping behind the cab at a distance. He has a snout now. I couldn't quite tell, but he seemed happy upon me discovering him.

Last I could remember of him up north, he wanted to kill me. Of all the others, he wasn't happy with our find. It's my guess that he regretted that night ever leading us there. I thought he fled west, after everything went wrong. Turns out I was wrong. He is obsessed with me. Once I get to the nearest hotel, I'm booking a room as fast as I can.

Entry 47

Safe. 27th week of my journey. Why did I come to this

city?

Entry 48

I walked out of my room this morning, to get food from the dining room. Getting into the elevator, when I closed the gate behind me, I saw Ezzy staring at me from the end of the hallway. Thank God the damned machine started moving.

Got what I needed. I had to run back to the elevator when I saw him coming down the stairs. When I was going up, I saw him turn around, almost immediately up the stairs. Strangest thing, nobody noticed Ezzy.

Entry 49

Cracking open the door, I can only see a face covered in long, dark fur, belonging to a body I can no longer describe, only his bloodshot eyes remain. I'm starting to hear whispering again, and not belonging to Ezzy. There seem to be more everywhere I listen. Outside my door, my window, from the walls. Every time I close my eyes, they seem to come closer until I sense the moving lips above my face. But when I open my eyes, the whispers move back to my door.

Whatever they all are, they have followed me here. I fear it now. I can't take it out of the sack. It seems to have gotten brighter.

Entry 50

A face is outside my window, and I have no curtains.

Entry 51

I cracked the door open again, and Ezzy was still there. Didn't see him for long, as I had to close and lock the door before he could budge his way in. At least he's not smiling anymore.

The face was not at the window today. That is, until I picked up the sack with it in it. Shadow appeared, and it was there. Strangely enough, I wasn't as scared as before. I don't know why, but I reached for it. Bring it out, thank God, the thing at the window shifted its gaze onto it, eagerly. The closest thing to peace, for at least it's not looking at me anymore.

Despite how hungry I am right now, I can't withstand not opening my door. The manager is bound to barge in now, any day.

I was a fool to take it with me. I can't remember why I took it, except it was so pretty.

Entry 52

It howls. They are responding. It howls, they howl, Ezzy howls. Never heard any sound like it, but a howl is the best I can call it.

It won't stop.

I'm going to gnaw off a finger. Nothing else to do. Goodbye, fleshy Robert. Pinky Andrew, you're next.

Entry 53

It's quiet. I checked the window. Only the gulf's waters to be seen. I've had enough. I'm leaving now, before it comes back.

Margrett, my love, you will not see me again. I am too far gone now, and it's better you remember me in memory anyway. You probably have been worried sick about where I've been. I hope it rests your heart to know I did not lose myself in those hills. However, of myself once I've finished, I don't know how I'll be. I've had to hide from them. I seem to have lost them, but they are aware of my presence in the area. I'm in the post office right now. I send this journal to you in hopes you'll have some idea what happened. Of what I uncovered, I discovered too late of its evil. I am cursed, Margrett. The eyes watch from the waters now, and these beasts have been following me, and what I carry. I'm going to destroy it. I have an idea how, but I must hurry before they find me here. I wish for your prayers, once you read this, that I may succeed. Don't go looking for me, I won't be in this place any longer. I'll find my peace either way. Forgive me. I pray God gives you only the brightest days in Virginia.

Love truly,
Teddy Grace

SUN STROKE

My name was Pan Hower. Beginning this piece, I should state the peculiarities and strangeness of this new land is of no surprise for people such as myself. Before traveling off from my family, I have learned of the stories, when told suddenly. They were an awakening to kindred.

As I once heard it described, a olden loose wrapped around our hearts. With utter fascination, we didn't bother ignoring the calls. As consequence, we split into our expeditions, from which for some the peculiarities showed themselves, such as the Almas, the Serbian Witchmen, and Francis's Wolf. I remember it like it was only a month. Strangely enough, when following the stories we became endowed with becoming a peculiarity ourselves, to our amusement.

From then on, we lived in our world, and everything became more faded, until the land we walked turned stranger. Fate we all were granted was now determined on the roll of the bone dice, under the madness of Catraunicus.

Some gave, some prospered, some weakened, some wizened, some maddened, some lived periodically. But then, some were given the unlucky side, like yours truly, and were, like some, expulsion. Didn't get to say my farewells to by grand-niece, but suspicions be, before the Ozark Howlers carry me off, he'll see me soon.

Crashing through the doors of a French church, I was on my first stop of the normalized world. Not even to this day do I remember what I may have done to cause such disturbance, but they would not have me there. Luckily, word didn't travel fast back then, and I was able to find shelter in a Spanish Monastery near the farther south along the gulf coast.

To my surprise, the peculiarities of this new land didn't die out yet, as I've had the luck or misfortune to come across the occasional Shifters migrating south. Settling down, I aged in this land, long enough to see the barren space around me turn into the Houston town it is presently.

One day, after deciding to finally break from the chapel of his benevolence, I walked down the road into the expansive cityscape. Continuing, I turn my head right, and spot a liquor store open for business. After some pondering then, I obliged, and stepped in to survey the stock. Moving around the shop, by complete chance I spotted my cousin Clouse at the counter, and I'd be darned to not say the dice played an interesting twist to my location just there.

There he was, mouthing off the store owner, oblivious to my being. Moving my gaze to the reflection of his face, I could see his dark whiskers as well as his yellow eyes buried under a furrowed brow.

Took him an hour to finish, when I finally greeted him in the dust of the road outside. I remember, such a wry smile crept on his face upon recognition. He never lost his peculiar state, even when the die was cast. Celebrations made, and soon we were collapsed amongst the tombstones, the stories retold, until the stars came and went.

As it turned out, Clouse came across the gray bushes a while back up in Kansas territory, stubbornly following in their path ever since. At the moment, to his knowing, what created them shouldn't be far from here. That was when I knew, the Ozark Howlers were near. Clouse wanted to carried off by them, and so did I.

We traveled westward, touched by the sun, watching our step in case white spots were in our path. Two days, then eight days. Trekking through the dry lands, before we finally found the gray bushes atop a rise near the base of a Mesa.

Not far off was our prize, father down along the sandy wall. Half-dead, Clouse and I ran. Then one of us stepped into a white spot, and the sands carried him off. Poor Clouse, his roll wasn't as lucky. It was a waste of a journey anyhow. The horned beast laying in front of me was dark furred and massive, its dog-like face turned away.

I was disgusted by the failure. The Ozark Howler, my chance, couldn't turn the body completely, and even now, is trapped in the bones of the host. The sun was touching my brain, and in my defeat I was nearly overtaken by heat sickness. I felt the hawks' laughter as they were above circling.

I looked down at the body again, and was unexpectedly hit with the question of why the compass of Great Mama was in its finger-like paws? Looking back at the decades, receiving the unlucky side, it's funny that I'm the first to find the exception.

In the end, I find myself on my own expedition, traveling the back roads of tar and dirt, compass in arms, and relieved. The Ozark Howlers have lost their way, but I know where they are now. The callings have been more frequent, showing themselves only as echoes of themselves. Restless, for we know I will have to search for assistance.

I pray to God that I carry on from this dreadful place.

THE HOMESTEAD ATTACK

On April 29 of 1922, the Jude family reported spotting a mysterious animal on their premises. Mr. Tom Jude, husband and father, reported on being woken up that morning at 5:30 by sounds of distress heard from his cattle.

Armed, Mr. Jude went outside and into the barn where his 30 cows were waiting to be milked, along with the family's one bull, penned to the side. Upon entering, amid the panicked livestock, Mr. Jude saw blood on a pillar of one of the stalls.

All of a sudden, as he put it, "a great animal bumped into me, and cut my leg deep before running past me into the pasture." According to the Mrs. Jude, she watched a large, dark predator run from the barn, and with brisk speed, turn toward the tree line.

When asked for a detailed description, Mr. Jude says that it looked like "some great cat with bulky features. Possibly a painter." Mrs. Jude, on the other hand, claimed to have gotten a clear view of the creature. "It first appeared to be a large boar or mountain cat. But as it was running I swear to the Lord that thing was a horned feline."

One cow was killed during the incident, and Mr. Jude is soon, reportedly, to have a swift recovery from the attack. While there is speculation of the details by council leaders in nearby Hatsbury, famers and other citizens of the county should be warned to keep a sharp eye out for any animal that may fit this description.

CONCATENATED

August 21, 1923

Dear Kevin Lindson,

It is with faith and trust in your secrecy that I provide you with this information gathered by the concatenations of Arkansas of the Concatenated Order of the Hoo-Hoo. This is an unofficial summary of the findings for the operation conducted by several other concatenations of our Order, as well as our own. With that knowledge, proceed to keep in privacy until delivered to the Arcade Building in St. Louis. The information shall only be shared with the Supreme Nine.

<u>Jonesboro:</u> After a periodical survey of the 10 mile radius over the last year, no sightings have been made. Final analysis being there are no sightings or activity near Jonesboro nor the northeastern sector.

<u>Stuttgart:</u> After a periodical survey o the 15 mile radius over the last year, no sightings have been made. Final analysis being there are no sightings or activity near Stuttgart.

<u>Warren:</u> After a periodical survey of the 20 mile radius over the last year, only a single sighting has been made near Farmville, by three of our members. Final analysis being suspected activity of a southern migration.

<u>Pine Bluff:</u> After a periodical survey of the 30 mile radius over the last year, there have been four sightings made near Redfield, Humphrey, and Grady by 15 of our members. Final analysis being suspected activity of a southern migration.

Malvern: After a periodical survey of the 30 mile radius over the last year, no sighting has been made. Final analysis being there are no sightings or activity near Malvern.

Camden: After a periodical survey of the 20 mile radius over the last year, no sighting has been made. Final analysis being there are no sightings or activity near Camden.

Gurden: After a periodical survey of the 30 mile radius over the last year, there have been 2 sightings near Curtis by five of our members. Final analysis being suspected activity of a southern migration.

Story: After a periodical survey of the 30 mile radius over the last year, there have been five sightings in the Ouachita National Forest near Rover and Harvey by eleven of our members, two of whom have been fatally attacked. Final analysis being suspected activity of a southern migration.

Springdale: After a periodical survey of 10 miles north and west, and 30 miles south and east over the last year, there have been two sightings near Forum and St. Paul by four of our members. Final analysis being suspected activity in the southern Ozark Mountains.

Mountain View: After a periodical survey of the 10 mile radius over the last year, no sighting has been made. Final analysis being there are no sightings or activity near Mountain View.

The surveys have been conducted by the concatenations of Little Rock, Pine Bluff, Warren, Malvern, Hot Springs, and Gurden. Overall conclusion being that judging from the survey locations, there are at least eight individual Ozark Howlers who have come down into our state of Arkansas from the Ozark mountain range.

The casualty rate has been low this year, but considering the Ozark Howlers moving south, I ask for the jurisdiction by the Supreme Nine to allow our members to fight back against these advances. I suggest the operation be taken to the next step forward, for the safety of regular people, and the secrecy of our organization's cause.

- Board of the Gurden Concatenation

THE HORNED MIRAGE

On the Eichbaum Road, it was the start of dawn when I rode down to the valley. It was quiet and empty, no one to be spotted on the horizon. Found my way through, after some time, and found myself in a shallow dip on the landscape. Sunbeams were touching the peaks off to my left side, and so I parked off road, and stepped out onto the dry earth.

Looking up at the point rise in front of me, I could see shadows grow and dance as the mountain was becoming an orange glow. By then, I was already trekking up the slope. For the rest of the morning I continued, with the sun at my back, and my neck a baked shade of brown.

As according to my watch, it was a little before noon when I finally settled against a red rock outcrop. I looked down from my position, down to the descending slope to where my car was resting, illuminated by the sun. It was a handsome sight. From up there, with nothing else but a faint wind, I witnessed strokes of orange, red, and gray painted upon that land. That was all I needed that day, ancient, merciless ruins. No sign of the living, no sign of movement, except for the retreating shadows on below cliff and mountain, and inside crevice.

One shadow in particular my was gaze was following. Slower than the rest, and I'd say a few dozen meters from the road toward the north east. Next thing I see, the shadows left it behind as the sun rose overhead. From where I sat, I was so far, and the figure's shape non-discernable.

I couldn't make sense of this strangeness. The heat was getting to me, so by then I knew I had to get back. I trudged down, made my way to my wagon, and cranked the engine. Even from my wagon, I could just see the dark shape in the distance. Thinking to myself, I decided to make my way over, last thing I'd do there for the day.

Getting closer, from my seat, there was more detail to be made.

I finally stopped, and looking upon what lay in front of me, I couldn't believe myself. I for sure was out there for too long, and I  should have left as soon as possible. But I paused, and instead stepped forward to the dry husk of a monster.

There was too much there. The skin like black leather, short tail, with dried out eyes in their sockets, and a build of a large dog, but many times as large. I only had to walk around to notice what looked like horns protruding from its head, and I knew for certain. I had found before myself a demon.

I immediately left it, and made sure to get out of that place. How did it up here on this Earth? That was it, the last I saw of that thing that did not belong there.

I was already there not even a day later, and it wasn't

there. No sign, not even bones. To this day, I don't understand what happened after I left. So far, there have not been others of its that I've seen. I'm relieved, thank god. Let Hell's spawn stay where they were born. They have no place here.

DAWSON'S TROPHIES

...as for my mama's side, they've tended to stick with their roots, being the northern foothills of the Ozark Mountains. Whenever there was a celebration, whether it's a family celebration, holiday, or a road trip up north, it was quickly learnt that you could only get a few of them to attend. Can't even remember their names, save for a few Angelas, Mollies, and Simons.

The only person I could really connect with was Uncle Paul. He was always the sort of person who was more sociable and amusing type, and would always have stories to tell everyone. He'd always come over when there's an opportunity, and was also the sort to not be shy of the big city, thank goodness.

According to mama, he has for a period been acquainted with city life, specifically along the West coast. But, as it seems to be for most of my family, there is no greater calling than the open air. There have also been periods where he seems have disappeared out of nowhere. I asked Uncle Paul this morning where he has been during those times, and he gave me the most absurd answer I have ever heard.

"I've been hunting Ozark Howlers."

I couldn't take him seriously after that. But he insisted, really insisted, that what he said was true.

"Every season, I'd pack up my things, go into those mountains, and shoot the little scoundrels. Small things they were. But those teeth, if I hadn't been careful, could have easily reached my throat, and left me for dead," he said. "But from what I learned, they hated the stench of

Whiskey, and preferred to hide in logs and cracks in the Mountains. So, what better way for your drunk uncle to get them little monsters than simply pouring Whiskey in their little hidey-holes, and picking them off when they ran?"

It was a good story, I'd give that to him. The stories about the Ozark Howler weren't uncommon to hear from mama's side, attacking cattle and living up in the mountains. But it was always understood by everyone as a rural legend. Indian myth.

"I got so good at it, that I've started clearing entire mountain, peak by peak, until last Spring. I couldn't find any of them left. I looked under logs, over pastures, poured whiskey everywhere I went for an entire month! But then I realized, there are no more Ozark Howlers to be hunted. Uncle Paul Dawson, killed them the Ozark Howlers till death they all parted!"

I'll tell you again, Uncle Paul is the amusing type. I love him lots, but he can be really ridiculous sometimes. Before we ended that conversation, he promised me that this fall, he will show me the pelts he collected. Wouldn't be surprised if they were mink skins. However, I'm sure there will be other things to focus on at his place.

William H. Dawson

FOLK CUSTOMS

The Ozarks may seem remote and isolated to the businessman sitting comfortably in his office in Atlanta, but historians of the area know that the people of Ozarks are descended from travelers from the four corners of the globe. British and Irish ancestry is well known, but French and Spanish influence is strong as well. African blood is known to be mixed in even with those residents who call themselves 'white', and of course the Indian strain remains.

The folkways of each of these groups are not as independent as they may seem. People talk to people, and share stories around the fire at night to keep off the dark, regardless of the racial boundaries that separate them while the sun is high.

So, local customs that reference the Ozark Howler seem to take on aspects the many ethnic groups that populate the hilly region. That said, there are some regional habits of life in the Ozarks that seem totally unconnected to any other practice, but are unique to the area. So it is with the daily routine of gestures, large and small, that the hill people practice in order to ward off the Ozark Howler, or to keep it in their favor, if possible.

The propitiation of the Ozark Howler takes place most often during times of transition. Upon undertaking a journey of unusual length, for example, the hill people will gather a few fistfuls of soil from near the foundation of their home, place the dirt into an empty cigar box or old tin, and wrap the container in a cloth that has been used for cleaning. Every few miles, a pinch of the soil is taken up in the left hand and cast by the side of the road, as the traveler mutters, "Howler be gone, I've still not left home."

Old timers say that after encountering the Ozark Howler, a person will suffer a kind of contamination. A man in this condition is described as "having the Howler on him". This impurity manifests itself in small, but frequent accidents such as minor stumbles, a propensity to break tools, as well as a propensity for forgetting important obligations. The remedy to "get the Howler off"

is to cover a stick with hog fat and give it to the family's dog. When the stick disappears, the bad luck will too.

Another anti-Howler hex has long served as a kind of capstone in Ozark funeral ceremonies. On the first full moon after a loved one has been buried, the eldest able-bodied woman in the deceased's household will return to the cemetery, and place a vine or supple green shoot from a tree, twisted into a shape reminiscent of an upside-down pretzel from Pennsylvania, atop the grave. In the western reaches of the hill, this same shape is made with flour. Every year, for the first five years after death, this symbol is laid down atop the grave again.

This practice stems from the association between the

Howler and passage into the realms of the dead. The approach of the Howler is said to be preceded by the sound of the tearing of cloth where there is no cloth being torn. This sound is in turn interpreted as an omen of death.

A single vision of an Ozark Howler is rare for anyone. A second sighting of it is believed to be a sign of good luck. However, this second sighting is received with foreboding as well, because to see the Howler a third time is a sign of certain death, soon to come.

This aspect of the Ozark Howler seems to have been derived from a combination of mythologies – those of the old as well as those of the new. A Cherokee legend tells a pair of old women who discovered the power to foretell death when they were out picking the berries of a yaupon holly bush, which were used in a ceremony to access the spirit world. Upon reaching the summit of a hill, where they knew a strong stand of yaupon to be, the pair came across a great black beast with red eyes the color of the fruit, eating the berries for itself. Surprised, the animal turned on the women, and struck them down, leaving the left cheek of each scarred for life. From that time forward, the women had the power to predict the death of any human being.

In Ireland, from where many European Ozark settlers came, there is a belief in the Cu Sith, a massive dog-like being that is one of the fairy people. The Cu Sith was said to appear to humans only as they approached death.

Similar to the Cu Sith are many other dark creatures said to populate the British Isles, such as the Moody Doo of the Isle of Man and the Boggart Dog of England. These beasts, descended from lore of the pre-Christian Celts, are described as large, with thick dark hair and glowing eyes, and to foretell the death of the person who sees them, or of a close family member.

The Ozark Howler's role as a messenger of death appears to be the result of the blending of these British creatures with Indian legends of a similar bent. Early European settlers encountering the stories of the people already here brought the two together, and gave them a twist of their own. Such is the case of so much of the American identity.

One of the novel turns in the Ozark Howler lore is the belief that the Howler visits the dead after they have passed. It is said that if the bereaved go to the grave of the departed in the three days after death, after dark, the Howler will be seen there, paying its respect, or perhaps guarding the grave. After those three days are over, however, the Howler will be seen no more.

It is also believed by some that when a young couple are parted by death before they can be married, the

surviving lover will hear the Howler's distinctive moan three times after all funeral rites and gatherings are done. The first howl is for what once was. The second howl is for what might have been. The third, longest howl, is heard only by those whose love ran true and deep. The third howl honors the moment of death, and calls the surviving lover to follow.

In the larger towns of the Ozarks, this lore of the three death howls has been shifted somewhat, so that now some people whose ancestors lived in the hills will talk about the three church bells of death. Still, they will refer to the old legends of the Ozark Howler without knowing they are doing so. Upon seeing a friend in grief, young women will say to each other, "The Howler is in the bell tower with her."

For those who hear the Ozark Howler and believe themselves doomed, however, there is a remedy. The curse can be throwed off by digging a trench in front of the door to a house, parallel to the house but not leading to it. At the bottom of the trench, a procession of flat stones must be planted, and then buried. This Howler Path is said to lead death to walk past the home, but not to enter it.

The question will occur to outsiders: How do these Ozark people know when the Ozark Howler is near, if the creature walks so stealthy in the night. The honest answer is that often, they do not know. Many times, they come upon the Howler when they least expect to see it.

However, there are some tricks for obtaining an early warning that are sworn by in some houses. One grandmother I spoke with showed me her Howler Bone, the wishbone of a chicken balanced on the lip of an old bottle of beer. When the bone falls from the bottle, she told me, it's a sign that the Howler is near.

Another woman told me about the Nightshade Doll, a craft that is woven from corn husks to take on the appearance of a young girl. The doll is hung securely in the branches of a tree, and when it is gone, the Howler is said to have paid a visit. The doll is irresistible to the monster, the woman claimed, but distracts it from its more predatory intentions. The doll seems to satisfy the creature's hunger in form, if not in substance.

Many people who have encountered the Hoo-Hoo and know its lore have a limited view of its beastly nature: It's a predatory animal, or at the very most, a carnivore with some odd, even supernatural characteristics. The point for these people is that the Howler is something completely different from themselves, something wild in nature and in habitat.

For others, the truth of the Ozark Howler is much stranger. The darkest secret of the Howler, as some tell it, is that the creature isn't really an inhuman monster after all. Instead, they say, the Howler is one of us, a human being that has somehow been changed into a beastly form.

How this happens is a matter of great dispute. There are those who say that a person is predisposed from birth to change into a Howler. Part of this predisposition is said to come from one's parentage, with certain families having a history of Howlering in their line. Astrology of a sort is also purported to play a role, although it's not of the zodiacal variety, but a more informal observance of "odd moons" foreboding a rather furry future for a newborn child.

The transformation into a Howler tends to come at the same time that other processes of physical maturation begin. When boys begin to get their beards and girls begin to get their curves, parents begin watching for signs of the feared additional change. The growth of a mole with hair coming through it is interpreted as one mark of a beast to come. Hair growing down the center of a young person's back is another.

Metamorphosis into an Ozark Howler isn't strictly restricted to adolescence, however. Any dramatic change of circumstances in life that leads a person to become socially isolated puts that person at risk of a change. In particular, widows and widowers are put under watch for several months after the funerals of their loved ones.

Another explanation is that people can be cursed, through malicious witchcraft, through possession of cursed objects, or through careless failure to observe certain "superstitious" practices. One of the stranger prohibitions in Ozark culture is the ban on planting cedar trees. It is supposed that a person who purposefully plants a cedar will change into a Howler within a month, unless the transplanted tree is ripped out and burned.

A person who becomes an Ozark Howler may be trapped in their new beastly form forever. However, there are also stories of people who go through certain periods as Howlers, only to return to their human form and re-enter society, as if they had been away on a long trip.

The Ozark Howler who is able to shift between animal and human shape at will is particularly feared. These Howlers are believed to be especially wicked, having chosen to become the vicious predators in the first place.

Why would a person choose to become an Ozark Howler? I have never found anyone who claims to have this power themselves, so the explanations I have are second hand speculations at best. Common knowledge supposes that people who become Ozark Howlers are somehow naturally shy of human company, and seek out quiet places away from social chatter. Some people say, though, that the desire to become an Ozark Howler has its origins in a simple delight in death and destruction, and a hatred for human expectations of moral behavior.

A few people question whether the Ozark Howler is actually as evil as it is generally believed to be. After all, the Howler generally keeps to itself, hunting other wild animals, much as humans often do. Those who are friendly to the Howler claim that it has never actually been caught attacking human beings, and say that any stories to the contrary are lies.

People who have such opinions usually keep them private, however. Suspicion falls upon those who fail to utter anything but contempt for the monster. They are accused of secretly being Howlers themselves, or of trying to protect family members who have undergone the transformation. Suspected Howlers, even if they appear to be completely ordinary human beings, are shunned by their communities.

There are a number of folk remedies that can be used to prevent the onset of a transformation into an Ozark Howler. A regimen of a weekly dose of goat's milk may be chosen, always administered on a Sunday morning. Alternately, a family may choose to banish its dogs from a hundred foot radius around the house for a week

before and a week after a young person's thirteenth birthday. An elixir containing the musk of a skunk is also given to children thought to be on the verge of the Howlering, though it is not certain whether the young ones feel that the protection is worth the ordeal.

Different parts of the Howler's body are said to confer medical benefits. An oil extracted from the greasy pieces of a Howler is said to relieve gout. The powdered claws of the creature are used to combat melancholy, while the powdered teeth are administered to heal broken bones. A soup made with the eyes of the Howler are said to convey the power to see into the future, although the eyes cease to glow with its death. The horns are the most sought after part of the beast, however, for they are used to cure impotence in the marital bed.

There are some people, among those who do not believe in the literal existence of the Ozark Howler, who assert that those who use these folk remedies are fools, for the parts traded as bits of the Howler's body are actually organs collected from different common animals, the teeth and claws from dogs, the horns from goats, and the Howler grease nothing but pig fat mixed in with a bit of dirt and horse hair for effect.

I will leave it up to others to determine the truth.

FOLK TALES

It's quite clear that few of the people who tell or hear these tales believe the stories to be true in a literal sense. Rather, they seem to take the popular belief in the Ozark Howler and play with it for the sake of entertainment, the sheer pleasure of spinning a nice, thick yarn.

THE STUBBORN NURSE

There was a family that lived a ways back on Souder Creek, and had a pretty little farmstead with a view up the valley that you couldn't rival anywhere else in the territory. It was a pretty little farm, with a pretty little farm wife, but the fact is that the crops weren't doing very well that year. Some say the farmer was busier with his wife than he should have been. Together, the pair of them had nine children living with them in their home, going all the way from a 16 year-old son to a baby girl.

It seemed like trouble was everywhere that year, and the worst of it began when the farm's oldest daughter, 12 year-old Rose Anne, went down the road to visit her friend. Springtime was making its way beautifully across the land, and Rose Anne was losing herself in the dogwood trees that were blooming all around her as she walked.

Maybe that was why she wasn't sure when it started following her. It was a big black thing, with a shoulder as high as her hat, walking right alongside her. It was nearly silent, but it had great big feet padding through the wildflowers by the side of the road.

Well, Rose Anne had never seen anything like it, but she had heard stories all right. She looked right at it, and it returned her gaze right back, with deep red eyes.

This girl had a strong mind, and she was determined not to show her fear. So, she stared straight ahead and continued to walk, as if nothing at all unusual was going on.

The beast wouldn't leave her, so after a while, she said aloud to it, "I figure you're that Howler I've heard about. That's fine with me, but I have some things to do today."

The beast said nothing. "All right," said Rose Anne. "It's agreed, and when we reach that big pin oak up there at the top of this hill I'll go my way and you will go yours."

When they reached the top of the hill, it happened just like that. The Howler turned away from the road and into the woods, and Rose Anne kept walking down that road by herself. When she returned home that evening, with an escort from her friend's father, she sat down with her family and told them all what had happened.

"That was well done, dear," said her mother. "The rest of you learn from her. If you should meet the Howler on the road, do just what she's done and I'm sure you will be fine."

That's just what happened. A few days later, Samuel, who was 14 years old, was sent to borrow some tools for his father, and along that same road, the Ozark Howler stepped out of the woods to walk alongside him.

Samuel would have been a fool not to be afraid, to be so close to such a big, strange thing as that, but he kept his head. If his younger sister could deal with it, so could he.

"I understand you've met my sister," he said, "and you deal with her well. My name is Samuel, and I would appreciate the same manners, if you are willing to give them."

The Howler nodded its head, and the two walked on for a while, until the beast left him at the top of the hill where the big pin oak grew.

So it happened that, by the end of the summer, all the children in the family met the Howler on their way. Well, all of them except that baby girl, who was too young to go walking down roads on her own like that, after all.

All seemed to go well, but at the end of the summer, the children, all except that baby girl who stayed close to her mother, took sick with a terrible fever. Miss Lincoln, a young woman from around the way, came in to the home as their nurse so that the sickness wouldn't spread any further.

Miss Lincoln had no patience for anything that wasn't directly connected with her job description. So, when the children in her care began to tell stories about the mighty Howler that visited them along the roadside, she sighed in obvious disapproval, and said, "There ain't no such thing as a Howler." That was the end of the conversation that day, as the children could that there would no convincing their nurse.

The nurse learned something quite different, however, as she was walking back to her parents' home for supper. At the bottom of the hill with the big pin oak tree at the top, the Howler came out of the woods and walked right alongside her. No one knows what either one of them was thinking at that moment, but as the approached the top, the Howler spoke, saying in a low but quite understandable voice, "There is such a thing. There is such a thing. There is such a thing."

Miss Lincoln had a stiff mind, but with enough humility to admit when she had made a mistake. So, the next morning, she told the children what had happened. A few told-you-sos were given, but it was Rose Anne who brought an end to the chatter as she asked the question that was on all of their minds. "What will you do if you meet it again?"

The response was certain. "I'll put him in my pocket is what I'll do. Now close your mouths and get some rest."

It was with less confidence that Miss Lincoln set her way on down the road at the end of the day. Still, she didn't hesitate in her step when the Howler joined her way up that hill as it had the day before. This time, when they approached the pin oak at the top, it said to her, "No pocket's fit for me. No pocket's fit for me. No pocket's fit for me." Miss Lincoln didn't try her hand at the match either.

When the nurse told the children what the Howler had said, they warned her urgently not to go home that night, but to stay with them in their house instead. She wouldn't abide it, and told them, "You hush, and I'll go where I please."

You can imagine how it went that evening. As the sun was setting, that stubborn Miss Lincoln set on down the road, though she knew what was waiting for her. The Howler came out of the wood just like it had before, and the nurse had a fair idea of what it would say before it did. "You'll go where I please. You'll go where I please. You'll go where I please."

Miss Lincoln did not anticipate what happened next, however. When they reached the pin oak at the top of the hill, the Howler did not turn to return to the wood, but dipped its head down to the nurse's ankles, placed its horns behind her knees, and with a flick of its muscular neck, flipped her up onto its great back, and ran on down the road at a speed which none could match.

That stubborn nurse did not return to her parents that evening, and was not to be found at the Souder Creek farm the next morning. No one ever saw her again.

Some might say she had it coming, but the innocents also paid a price for her insolence at the Howler. Without a nurse to tend to them, those children were all dead of the fever within a week. All except that baby girl, that is, who grew up into a fine woman and still lives on that farm to this day, but has never taken one step on a walk down that road.

THE OZARK HOWLER BUYS A BANJO

One summer, there was this man who said he came from Kansas City, and he walking all over the countryside, taking orders for musical instruments. The only instrument that he actually brought with him as he walked around from home to home, though, was a banjo. I guess someone told this fellow that we all play the banjo around here. Me, I prefer the fiddle.

Anyway, this guy came up the road one day and my neighbor, Mr. Talbot, decided to have a bit of fun. The salesman comes walking up, carrying his banjo under his arm, pointing it at the ground like it was a loaded rifle. Mr. Talbot was just sitting on his porch, enjoying some shade in the afternoon sun. So, the salesman asked my neighbor whether he has any need for musical instrument. Mr. Talbot says no he doesn't, "But that's a mighty fine banjo, I need like to take a closer look."

Mr. Talbot played few notes, but the thing wasn't in tune at all. He handed the banjo back to the salesman, saying "I don't need a banjo, but there is a fellow right up over the hills from here who just lost his banjo in a house fire, and could use another one real bad." Well, the salesman knew what a prospect sounded like for sure, so he asked for the name of the man who needed the banjo.

Now I don't know what entered Mr. Talbot's head to say this, but I don't pretend to understand the mysteries of men's souls. He said, "The man you're looking for is someone we call the Ozark Howler." The salesman was kind of stumped at that. "What's the man's actual name?" the salesman asked.

"I couldn't tell you that," said my neighbor, "because I don't know. No one does. Or, at least, nobody remembers. He's an old fellow who's been living up in the hills for as long as anyone can remember, and playing his own strange kind of music there too. Why, I think if you keep on walking, you're guaranteed to hear his music tonight."

Mr. Talbot pointed the salesman in the right direction, up into the hills. The salesman thanked him, and went on his way, and I do believe that he was whistling a happy tune.

At a crossroads about an hour later on up the way, the salesman came to the house of Mrs. McDaniels. Her husband died a year previous, and she was struggling mighty hard, taking care of her four young children. So, when she saw the salesman walking up the path that day, she knew what trouble looked like. She did her best to ignore his persistent questions, but he just didn't give up. He kept on asking her if she knew which way to go to find the Ozark Howler.

He said he needed to sell the Howler a banjo, and as if to illustrate his point, he began to play at the banjo. To say that Mrs. McDaniel had never heard such a thing before, is not a compliment. The man's fingers certainly moved quickly enough, but any fool could tell that the banjo was out of tune. Apparently this salesman was not just any fool.

Well, Mrs. McDaniels figured that as long as this man was there bothering her And making a racket, he might as well make himself useful. "So," she said, "if you really want to know where the All-Star collars, I'm going to need some time to check with my neighbor, Miss Reynolds."

"I'll make you a deal," Mrs. McDaniel said. "if you set to washing those dishes there in that sink, by the time you're done I'll be back and I'll tell you where you can find the Howler. So, Mrs. McDaniel's walked out the back door and over and around the corner, as if she was going off to see your neighbor, but found herself a comfortable place to lie down and take a much-needed nap instead. After about a half an hour, She woke up, feeling much better, and went back inside. The salesman was just finishing up on a very greasy pan.

"I talked to Mrs. Reynolds," she said, "and my friend tells me that the Ozark Howler, if you're looking for him, was last seen over on the other side of the waterfall about two miles up over that way. You'll know you're close to the waterfall when you hear the sound of the water. Cross the stream on top, and watch your footing so you don't slip. And then you're going to find the home of Mr. Samuel. Now, Mr. Samuel doesn't like to talk much, but he could show you the way to the Howler better than anyone."

Now, when Mrs. McDaniel said that Mr. Samuel wasn't very talkative, she was telling the half of it. The truth was, he had never spoken a word in his whole life. Some people said he was a mute, but I'm betting he was just plain stubborn.

Well, a couple hours later, with his pants soaked all the way through from walking through the creek, the salesman came up to Mr. Samuel's cabin, still carrying that banjo of his. The sun was setting by this time, but the afternoon had heated up something awful, so he caught his breath and had a drink of water before asking Mr. Samuel if he could please tell him where he would find the Ozark Howler. Mr. Samuel just looked at him kind of funny, as if the salesman was asking the stupidest question ever heard.

"I heard the Ozark Howler needs a banjo," said the salesman. Mr. Samuel cocked his head to the side and opened his mouth half way, as if he was about to speak, as if something was provoking him to, after all these years, finally let loose his tongue. Mr. Samuel did not let that temptation run away with him however. He remained silent.

The salesman responded by taking out the banjo, and trying to play a tune. The sound was as awful as ever, with each string refusing to acknowledge the pitch of the others. Mr. Samuel didn't clap. He didn't tap his foot or snap his fingers. He just stared at the attempted performance with unrelenting wonder. After going through a few broken verses, his fingers gave out, and he could only stare at his ornery audience in return.

Five minutes passed this way, with neither man speaking, and neither man moving. Sitting on the rail of Mr. Samuel's front porch, the salesman felt the heat of the summer afternoon soak into him. The harsh hum of the cicadas blended with the rhythm of his mind, until he nearly fell asleep.

After an eternal moment, the salesman jerked his head back into full consciousness, cleared his throat and asked for help a third time. "I really would like to know where I could find the Ozark Howler, and if you would help me I would be much obliged to you," he said. Mr. Samuel didn't say a thing, but stomped his left foot and pointed with his big dirty pointer finger up to the top of the mountain behind his house. Well, the salesman knew when he was done with a pitch, so he just picked up his banjo and with the shadows of Twilight gathering around him, began his hike up the mountain.

That was the last that anyone ever saw of the man from Kansas City who was selling musical instruments. Nobody ever found a trace of him, but the next day, Mrs. McDaniels did take a walk with her children up to check on Mr. Samuel and see what had become of the salesman.

Mr. Samuel, characteristically, had nothing to say on the matter, but Mrs. McDaniel did notice that her neighbor was playing a brand new banjo, and my goodness if it didn't look exactly like the one that the salesman had held in his hand the day before. As Mr. Samuel plucked away at it, she was pleasantly surprised to hear that the instrument had finally been tuned.

THE BLACK HOWLER OF FALLING SPRING

Wander a half mile south of Wildcat Hollow, you'll find a secluded little spot with a mill pond constructed where water flows freely from the hillside. The people who live in the area have a story about the place, and the girl who was unwise enough to become familiar with the Howler who lived nearby.

The story has it that at this site generations ago, there lived a miller who, though once successful, had known only hardship since his wife died giving birth to their third daughter. The miller had three daughters, and though he was thankful for their company, he worked himself close to exhaustion trying to keep them clothed and fed.

The girls would play by the pond, which in the way of imaginative children they had given a fanciful name. The Wishing Pond, they called it.

The name arose from a habit the girls had since they could remember. They would sit at the pond's edge, in a spot where a big, flat, comfortable rock came out of the hillside a few feet above the water. From this angle, they could see the reflections of the area around the pond when the wind was still, but in a strange, distorted way.

This place, the girls decided, was made for wishing. That's what they would do there most days, making wishes before it was time for them to prepare dinner. You can imagine what kind of wishes the three of them made, never really expecting them to come true.

One day, however, that changed. Clara, the oldest of the sisters, was preparing for her 16th birthday, and the two youngest girls, both excited and jealous, decided to respond to the upcoming event by teasing her.

As they lay on the rock together in the warm springtime sun, the youngest sister began. "I wish today for a mysterious stranger to visit the mill," she said.

"Yes," said the middle child. "That's a good wish, but I'll add my wish onto yours. I wish that the mysterious stranger comes carrying flowers."

The girls shared more than a few giggles about that, but the laughing stopped when the youngest sister said, "I bet I know what you're going to wish for, Clara. You'll wish that this mysterious stranger asks you to marry him."

"Don't be absurd," Clara responded.

"Oh yes," said his sisters. "We know how much you dream about him coming to take you away so that the two of you can kiss without papa interrupting you."

"You don't know what you're talking about," Clara said seriously. "You aren't old enough to remember what happened to mama because of all that kissing. Besides, I'm too picky to let any mysterious stranger come along and marry me just like that."

Clara decided to tease her sisters back, and with a mischievous look in her eye, she continued. "The truth is, I've already found my true love. He lives right close by, so that when we do get married, I can come visit you whenever I like."

The younger girls fell for her story right away, so eager they were to see anything new and exciting enter their lives. "Who is he?" they asked.

"Well," said Clara, "he's big and strong, and he's got thick black hair, and he does whatever he wants, and always he gets away with it too."

"How long have you been seeing him?"

"Oh, I've only seen him a couple of times, but I know he likes me. Everyone around here knows him."

Her sisters begged over and over for his name, but Clara refused to say anything for the longest time, until she could see that it was time for them to return to the house.

"All right, but I'm telling you, you'll be shocked. He's a very unusual character. The only one I will ever wish to marry," she said, now speaking very slowly so as to prolong the suspense, "is the Black Howler that lives in a cave at the top of a hill just over yonder."

Her little sisters were screaming with an entertaining combination of fear and amusement at the idea. So, Clara kept the story going just to prolong the moment.

"Yes, it's true," she said. "We've already made plans. I do believe he'll come by to pick me up this very evening. Now come along. It's time we go."

This silly conversation was all but forgotten by the time that dinner was finished, and the girls joined their father by the fire as he smoked his pipe. Barely had they taken a seat when there came a loud knock on the door.

"Maybe it's a mysterious stranger," said the youngest daughter.

"Maybe he's carrying flowers and will ask Clara to marry him," said the middle sister.

"Maybe he'll walk away if somebody doesn't go answer the door," Clara said, and went over to open the door.

It was already twilight, and so no one could say exactly what they saw outside the door that evening. One thing was for certain, however. It was no human being that stood out there in the dusk.

It was a dark beast with thick black hair all over its body, a pair of horns on top of its head, and two glowing red eyes fixed on Clara. Oddest of all, it had what looked like a garland of wildflowers hanging from its horns.

To the surprise of everyone, the beast spoke. "I've come for you Clara, just as you said I would. Will you go with me?"

Without a moment's hesitation, Clara ran forward and leaped up onto the creature's back. Without an explanation or even a goodbye, the thing turned and ran, fast as any horse, away into the gathering gloom.

I would like to tell you that Clara escaped somehow, or at least that the miller and his two younger daughters never saw Clara again. That, however, would be a lie.

Every now and then, for years afterward, especially in the springtime, one of the family members would come home saying that they had just seen Clara, dressed all in white, standing on a nearby hill, or across the little river, standing gazing up at the sky, or gathering plants. A couple of times, the miller saw her wave at him.

They would call after her, of course, and try to get to where she was. Before they could reach her, however, she would disappear, and there wouldn't be a trace of her having been there at all.

The three had to admit that she did not look unhappy. Still, they missed her terribly. Every now and then, the family would leave small packages of food in the places they had seen Clara. She didn't seem poorly fed, but they thought she might miss the taste of home.

After that day that the Howler came to take her away, Clara's sisters never made another wish on the millpond again.

Would you?

THE SNAWFUS AND THE HOWLER

On a dark night with the mists of the hills gathered close, a person can easily slide into a terrified silence, haunted by regrets and gloomy premonitions, listening for the approach of doom through the shadows. The very land itself feels like a curse, soaked in the knowing of a man's secrets, his betrayals, his failed courage. These were the thoughts that stuck in the mind of Jim Clifton the night he met the Howler a second time.

He had never forgotten their first meeting, though for ten years he had struggled to put it out of his mind.

Sometimes, in moments when the sun was gentle in its warmth and the breeze lifted him forward rather than bearing down on him, he thought it might be possible to leave it behind.

These were, however, only moments. He knew by now that the weight would never leave him.

He had been 14 years old, working with his father cutting and hauling lumber for a new project on the farm. What the project would be, Jim didn't know yet.

"One step at a time," his father told him. "First let's get our last load back home."

They had spent the day cutting a stand of big cedar, as thick around as could be found, his father said. The first loads were easy, and Jim felt his young strength with the pride of someone who felt like a man for the first time in his life.

As they returned for the last logs, however, the sky had turned dark, and rain had begun to fall, thunder booming in the distance. The wagon had a new creak to it, after a day's heavy loads, and Jim's confidence had left him, to be replaced with a clinging sense of unease.

Jim had asked his father if they might just make the last run early in the morning, but he knew what the response would be even before it left his father's mouth. "No," was the reply. "A job left unfinished stays unfinished. There's always a good reason not to get it done, once the delays start."

So, they went back to the cedar stand to fetch their last load, but now, what had been a dry track had become mud, and just around the final corner before their destination, the wagon became stuck. For a good hour, Jim and his father worked to get the wagon free as darkness fell around them.

Finally, they pulled free and lurched forward. That's when it hit.

One moment, his father was sitting beside him on the bench with the reins in his hands. The next, he was down in the mud, screaming, with something on top of him, ripping.

It was just a brief flash of lightning to show him what was there, but it remained in his mind like a photograph. A creature pinned his father to the ground with massive front legs carrying the weight of a huge body, covered with thick fur. In the brilliance of the bolt from the skies, two twisting horns rising from the beast's head glistened with rain as it arched its neck back to howl.

Jim didn't think. He didn't try to fight the beast. He urged the already terrified horses into a run, the empty wagon bouncing along the track behind them. He rode on the power of their fear, without the strength to direct them, allowing them to find their own way back home.

Jim never saw his father again – never even spoke of him again. Men from other families found the body, in pieces, the next day, and put together a scenario that was likely enough: A bear attack. He heard their words of reassurance, but knew it was no bear that took his father down.

Now, a decade running from that night, he found himself in the same spot. How? A wrong turn here and there, lost in thought as he rode back on a rare visit to his mother, and he had arrived, his horse stopping of its own accord in the middle of the overgrown path.

The feeling seemed to roll through him that he must be here to join his father, that he had been in flight ever since that night, as if he were prey, unthinking still, and now in the presence of his pursuer could do nothing but offer his surrender.

Stepping down to the ground, Jim felt it give way under his weight, soft from a recent rain. Stepping forward into the brush, he pushed away the branches of young cedar trees and tripped over the stump still standing of their ancestor, a victim of his father for a project that would never begin.

Jim heard it approach, moving through the

undergrowth ahead. This time, he knew he would not flee. This time, he would be taken.

He lowered his gaze as he heard the subtle sounds of the animal's approach. He saw with clarity the green carpet on which he stood, the shoots of green grass and horsetails pushing through the earth, his hand resting on the moss stretching itself softly over an ancient stone.

Jim heard his predator push through the undergrowth not ten feet in front of him, and stop. He shook with the same fear he felt as a boy, but would not move. Ten minutes might have passed before he lifted his head to meet the creature's gaze.

When he did, what he saw before him was not the savage dark predator he expected. Instead, before him towered a stag, the tallest he had ever seen, covered in a coat of white fur so pure, so unmarked by any stain that it seemed to glow even in the daylight, reflecting back even more of the brilliance of the sun than it received. Atop its head was a broad set of antlers with many points. Yet, these antlers were not hard and barren, but supple, and from them grew the leaves and pink white blossoms of a dogwood tree in springtime.

Before Jim could grasp what he was seeing, the stag opened its mouth, and without a sound exhaled a thick blue mist that flowed all around them, covering every inch of them in a delicious, cool moisture.

What was it that Jim felt in that moment as he breathed in that mist? Was it relief? Release? Forgiveness?

No. It was nothing less than the feeling of being alive after ten years underground.

At dusk, opening the door of his mother's house, Jim finally told her what had really happened the night she lost her husband. He told her what he had done, and what he had not done, how he had left his father behind, saving himself. He told her about the white stag he had seen that afternoon, about the flowers on its antlers, and its clean, cool breath.

Jim's mother reached up from her chair to pull him down onto his knees before her, her arms drawing around his shoulders. "I know," she whispered. "I always knew."

"What you met today," she said, "Is the Snawfus. It's the spirit of these hills from before our people ever came here to clear the land. But then, so is the beast that killed your papa, the Howler."

"We can't have one without the other," she continued, "any more than we can have day without night, love without loss, life without death."

She pulled him in even closer, until he could feel the hot breath of her words on his neck. "Every son leaves his father behind," she said. "and if you stay in these lands long enough, your son will do the same. It's not your place to decide when the Howler comes for you, but he will. He comes for us all."

"In the meantime," she continued, "walk with the Snawfus when you can."

There was nothing more to be said. So, his mother led Jim to the table, and fed him a thick stew, and sent him off to bed. In the morning, he awoke, unburdened.

POETRY

The Ozark Howler is undeniably strange. It defies the expectations we have both for man and for beast. Perhaps this is why several people have written poems about the Ozark Howler. We require unusual language to write about such an unusual creature.

I have noticed that those who write poetry about the Ozark Howler are those who stand awkwardly at the crossroads of traditional rural life and the opportunity presented by formal education, a ticket to a wider world. It is as if these poets seek to introduce the strange monster of their roots to the less shadowy world of paved roads, of automobiles, of news from far cities.

Are they reluctant to expose their shadow to the light of day, for fear it would disappear? I have tried to create a record of the more direct spoken and written words shared about the Ozark Howler, but am compelled to conclude this book with a few verses written to communicate the feeling as well as the facts about the beast.

ROCK OF COMFORT

This poem was given to me by Dennis Murphy, a young professor aspiring to write the epic of the Ozarks. The project seems like Odysseus, always on the verge of beginning a true effort to navigate home, only to meet frustration in the form of local monsters and distracting intoxications. He promises more, but for now, Murphy has offered this poem, a retelling of the imagery of a story he told me about the origin of the Ozark Howler's distinctive cry, included earlier in the book.

Twisted rope, sleeping child
Waiting in the subtle night
Rising to the hilltop wild
Men withdraw, time is tight.

Abandoned to the elements
No family will offer twice
Withholding ancient arguments
Of necessary sacrifice

Without this beastly drunken meal
A creature who delivers death
Red eye and horn and toothy zeal
Would seize each frontiersman's last breath.
They crossed the river making claim
Not knowing what was living there
They crossed its path and learned the names
Of Hoo-Hoo and the Nightshade Bear.

Each year like Abraham they give
Appointed by the mortal clock
A younger soul so they may live
To see the blood on Comfort Rock.

When will the men refuse to bend
To fear of stronger beasts than they

And come together to defend
Their sons and daughters on that day?

Come hunt the hunter, take your gun
And offer it a poisoned bowel
A hidden gift of venom won
To give the Ozark hills their howl.

THE STRAW GIRL

This poem was written by a 16 year-old girl for her school's competition in Mammoth Spring, a town on the border of Missouri and Arkansas. Though she remained with her aunt and uncle there during the week, she still returned to her parents' rural outpost outside Koshkonong, a few miles to the north from there.

She told me of the stories her family shared with her of times when families lost their children to the appetite of the Howler, and of the courage it took for her simply to go outside to use the outhouse after hearing these tales. It was clear to me that she imagines herself as the straw girl, with an intense personality that may go up in flames at any moment.

Bundle up straw from last harvest
                with the strongest twine,
Tie as tight as you would your life as I will hold mine,
Bind the bundles to my body until I'm covered fair,
With only my eyes to see what's out there,
Dry straw crackling as I'll bend my joints
                from underneath I'll hide,
The armor keeping in my fear, as I'll go
                straight on outside,
Marching on in perfect line past the doorway
                and to the fields I'll go,
Sunbeams reaching out to me making
                my new complexion glow,
The straw girl is not breakable
                the straw girl isn't scared
The straw girl gives herself to harvest
                so the village can be spared
Is what I'll tell myself when I cross
                the field and approach the wood
Remembering what my pa told me of
                what it is I should;

Walk on straight, and don't be scared,

Face the devil, and you may be spared,
Go farther out than you've ever been,
Go climb up the nearest mountain,
When the time comes, don't be scared,
Face the devil, you may be spared

Remembering what my pa told me of
                        what it is I should,
I'll continue deeper and deeper into the wood,
Until night falls, when I'm on the mountain,
I will make sure to keep my scattering thoughts in,
When night falls, and I lay down in
                        my armor of dry straw,
I'll make sure to listen for the beast's long claws,
And when in my vision its red eyes
                        and horns come into sight,
The straw girl will not, will not scream in fright,
Even as it approaches, with its large feline form,
I will turn away, and wish for none to mourn,
For the straw girl is not breakable
                        the straw girl isn't scared,
The straw girl will give herself to harvest
                        so the village can be spared,
For the rest of the season, every family will
                        breathe in peace,
By a howl's blessing, the straw girl will be released,
And join with her straw sisters, as the new centerpiece,
In the churchyard, I will wave
                        goodbye to god's subjects,
And with my sisters, waiting to see who's next.

ON THE BRINK OF A ROCK

The broken village of Ox's Rock,
And a tiny small home,
A morning's clock,
They brought a child's time alone

T'was silent and alone,
Till he heard the beasts groan,
Running towards home for safety,
Couldn't see the beast's hide among the spruce trees

Realized he was lost among the forest oaks,
The boy ran and ran,
Trying to find his folks

Cornered on a cliff, he scanned
                    the surrounding bushes,
Hoping for closure, but the beast pushes

Falling, he could only hope he would magically rise,
Last thing he saw were the eyes

SAUL ASHTON

THE HOWLER AIN'T

This poem is actually the lyrics to a song, which I have heard sung here and there throughout the region in differing versions. It was originally published in print in the Ozark Songbook a few years ago, and was first recorded on a farm near Dryfork, Arkansas.

The Black Howler
It ain't no dog.
I'd sooner say it's a giant frog
Sitting and howling on a log.

The Black Howler
It ain't no cat.
I never seen a kitty with horns like that
It could eat my tabby in seconds flat.

The Black Howler
It ain't no bear
A long tale like that you've seen nowhere.
Jumped right out at me, gave me a scare.

Oh Ozark Howler, just stay away.
Oh Ozark Howler, don't come around today.

RED

This colorful poem was shared during a seminar of young writers at Southeastern Missouri College that I had the honor to visit as I was researching this book. I am not certain whether its composition was provoked by the news of my imminent arrival. In any case, the timing was fortuitous.

The color of an osier twig, young in the springtime,
Of rare gems out of the earth and polished clean,
Of signs that seek to block my way,
Of well-weathered barns atop unnamed hills,
Of newts,
Of fruits,
Of the old leaves in autumn that fed their roots,
But which of these do we see signified in the eyes of the
Black Howler
Glowing in angry contradiction of its matted fur?
None at all.
It's the blood flowing through its cursed body that we see,
Nourished by those who have fallen to its dread
Hot and steaming in the cool night air.
It is a creature of scarlet riven rivers,
Turning our gaze against us.

ABOUT THE EDITOR

Hawthorne Cornus was born unexpectedly in Marble Falls, Arkansas, which is to say that he was not really born in anything other than the back of his parents' station wagon. His mother repeatedly has reminded Hawthorne that there was no anaesthesia or medical attention involved in the birth, and so Hawthorne has come to feel that his injuries are rarely worthy of care, resulting in a tendency toward festering. His interest in the Ozark Howler stems from the stories told to him by friends of his parents, in half apology, a feeling of sad self-mockery. He aims to give the lore of the Ozarks the respect it deserves, but fears that this mission will be harmed by his ridiculous name, the great joke of being named after two trees growing near the place of his birth, which was the location for several awkward birthday gatherings during his youth.